AN ENSIGN TO ALL PEOPLE

AN
ENSIGN
TO ALL
PEOPLE

The Sacred Message
and Mission of the
Book of Mormon

Monte S. Nyman

Deseret Book Company
Salt Lake City, Utah

First printing March 1987

Library of Congress Cataloging-in-Publication Data

Nyman, Monte S.
　　　An ensign to all people.

　　　Bibliography: p.
　　　Includes index
　　　1. Book of Mormon—Criticism, interpretation, etc.
2. Book of Mormon—Theology. I. Title.
BX8627.N95 1987　　　289.3'22　　　87-494
ISBN 0-87579-074-4

Contents

Preface

In a revelation given to the Prophet Joseph Smith almost two and a half years after the publication of the Book of Mormon, the Lord said that the members of The Church of Jesus Christ of Latter-day Saints were under condemnation because they had "treated lightly the things [they had] received." The Lord said: "They shall remain under this condemnation until they repent and remember the new covenant, even the Book of Mormon and the former commandments which I have given them, not only to say, but to do according to that which I have written." (D&C 84:54-57.) President Ezra Taft Benson has stated for years that the Church remains under condemnation because the members still do not use the Book of Mormon as the Lord would have them use it.[1] In the first general conference under his administration, this modern prophet, seer, and revelator proclaimed that the Church could be delivered from condemnation by the proper use of the Book of Mormon:

> The Lord inspired His servant Lorenzo Snow to reemphasize the principle of tithing to redeem the Church from financial bondage. In those days the General Authorities took that message to the members of the Church.
>
> Now, in our day, the Lord has revealed the need to reemphasize the Book of Mormon to get the Church and all the chil-

dren of Zion out from under condemnation—the scourge and
judgment. (See D&C 84:54-58.) This message must be carried
to the members of the Church throughout the world.

President Benson concluded that conference with a blessing
and promise:

> I bless you with increased discernment to judge between
> Christ and anti-Christ. I bless you with increased power to do
> good and to resist evil. I bless you with increased *understanding*
> of the Book of Mormon. I promise you that from this moment
> forward, if we will daily sup from its pages and abide by its pre-
> cepts, God will pour out upon each child of Zion and the
> Church a blessing hitherto unknown—and we will plead to the
> Lord that He will begin to lift the condemnation—the scourge
> and judgment. Of this I bear solemn witness.[2]

There are undoubtedly several reasons why members of the
Church do not use the Book of Mormon the way they should, but
one of the major reasons is probably that they do not understand
the significance of this great latter-day volume of scripture. They
fail to see the book's unique role in the Church and in the world.
Its value was declared by the prophet Joseph Smith: "Take away
the Book of Mormon and the revelations, and where is our religion? We have none."[3] In support of the prophet's statement, an
analysis of the early revelations given to him shows that each of
the first twenty sections of the Doctrine and Covenants relates in
some way to the coming forth of the Book of Mormon as a marvelous work and a wonder. They are discussed in chapter 1.

The purpose of this work is to show the importance the Book
of Mormon has in the eyes of the Lord and of his prophets. By
realizing how important the Book of Mormon is to the Lord Jesus
Christ, members of the Church may be encouraged to read it, to
follow its teachings, and to use it in proclaiming the gospel.

Also, I want to show how the Book of Mormon is an ensign to
the nations and how it was brought forth by a choice seer, Joseph
Smith. This is discussed in chapter 2.

One role of the Book of Mormon is to gather Israel in the latter days. Ancient Israel was scattered among all nations. The
prophets foretold that scattered Israel would be gathered again.

The allegory of the olive tree is a prophetic overview of the scattering and gathering. A detailed study of that allegory comprises chapter 3.

John the Revelator proclaimed that the book was to go to every nation, kindred, tongue, and people. (Revelation 14:6.) The Book of Mormon declares that various nations will have the opportunity to receive its message and notes what will be accomplished. Chapters 4 through 8 discuss the role of the Book of Mormon to the various nations.

Finally, the culmination of the nations' hearing the gospel through the Book of Mormon will result in the building of the two cities of Zion, the New Jerusalem and Jerusalem, the culmination of an ensign being lifted to the nations. The Book of Mormon teachings on this subject are discussed in chapters 9 and 10.

I would like to thank Eleanor Knowles and the Deseret Book staff for their constructive criticism, and Charles D. Tate, Jr., for his editorial assistance in bringing the manuscript into its final form. I would also like to thank my wife and family for their patience and encouragement in the preparation of this work.

1

An Ensign to the Nations

An ensign is a flag or a sign that symbolizes a nation, a school, or a specific group and is a signal or rallying point to other nations, schools, or groups. Today the Church is an ensign to all people in drawing their attention to the restoration of the gospel. Since that restoration, the Book of Mormon has been an ensign to draw the attention of believers in Christ and gather them together so that the Church might grow and flourish. When the Church has progressed sufficiently to establish a Zion people and to build a literal city of Zion, as foretold in the scriptures, that city will become an ensign to the political nations of the earth. (Isaiah 61:1-3.) Since the Book of Mormon is an initial ensign of the restoration and is the ensign that will open up each nation to the establishment of the Church, it is imperative to understand its role in gathering people together to establish the Church and eventually the city of Zion.

The Book of Mormon is basically an account of the ancient inhabitants of the Americas, but it also contains the Lord's word and thus is an ensign to the people of every nation in these latter days. The account was recorded on metal plates by prophets and apostles among the ancient inhabitants of the Americas. These plates were shown in 1823 to a young man named Joseph Smith in the state of New York by one of those ancient prophets named Moroni, a resurrected being. (JS–H 1:30.) Moroni was the last prophet to write upon those plates and was instructed by the Lord to reveal their whereabouts to Joseph Smith.

After four years of intense preparation, Joseph was entrusted with the plates and commissioned by the Lord to translate the record. (JS–H 1:53-54, 59.) With the aid of a urim and thummim that had been deposited with the plates[1] and by the gift and power of God, Joseph was able to render the record into English from a language called reformed Egyptian. (Mormon 9:32-34.) The completed translation was published as the Book of Mormon, being named after Moroni's father, Mormon, who had recorded most of the account upon the plates that were translated.

Joseph Smith was given several revelations by the Lord to prepare him for and encourage him in his work of translation. In a revelation given in March 1829, just prior to the time when the major part of the translation was begun, the Lord revealed that "this [our] generation" would have the word of the Lord through Joseph Smith. (D&C 5:10.) I believe that in the context of the revelation, the word of the Lord is the Book of Mormon. In the same revelation, the Lord noted that other things were reserved for future generations. (D&C 5:9.) Only part of the record was translated, because part of it was sealed, and Joseph was commanded not to translate the part that was sealed.[2] The portion that was translated was to be the Lord's guideline for his people until future generations would be given more. The generation referred to is undoubtedly all the people from the time the Book of Mormon was translated and published until the generation when the Church will so use the Book of Mormon that the Lord will reveal the sealed portion.

The prophets of the Old Testament had foreseen the restoration of this great and marvelous work, this ensign, and rejoiced in what is promised.[3] The ancient American prophets had also seen the restoration of Christ's true church to the earth and had been promised that their words, those on the records, would come forth in the latter days. (Enos 1:15-18.) As the Lord prepared Joseph Smith to translate the plates, He stated in a revelation that the visions and promises to these ancient prophets were now about to be fulfilled. (D&C 10:46-52.) A study of the Lord's words to Joseph Smith and to Isaiah about the Book of Mormon verifies that the

Book of Mormon does indeed fulfill the Lord's promise. The Book of Mormon is called in these sources "an ensign," "a marvelous work and a wonder," "a standard," or "a banner." And it is just that, as a careful analysis will show.

The prophet Isaiah spoke repeatedly of an "ensign" that was to be lifted up to the nations. (Isaiah 5:26; 11:10, 12; 18:3.) The Hebrew word for ensign is *nes,* and it is elsewhere translated in Isaiah as "banner" (Isaiah 13:2) and "standard" (Isaiah 49:22; 62:10). I believe that in most of these scriptures, the word *ensign* refers to the Book of Mormon specifically, and that when it is not specific, it refers to the Church or the work that will grow out of the coming forth of the Book of Mormon.[4]

In the Book of Mormon, the Lord promised Nephi and his father, Lehi, that their words and those of their seed would "proceed forth" out of his mouth to their descendants and that his words would "hiss forth" to the ends of the earth, for a standard or an ensign to his people, which were of the house of Israel. (2 Nephi 29:2.) Note that the Lord quoted Isaiah almost verbatim. Isaiah 5:26 says the Lord would lift an ensign to the nations from afar and would hiss unto them from the ends of the earth. The Lord designates the Nephite's words, the Book of Mormon, as a standard (or ensign) for his people. He also told Nephi that he would do a marvelous work "at that day" when he remembered his covenants to set his hand again the second time to recover his people, who are of the house of Israel. (2 Nephi 29:1.) This marvelous work and a wonder includes the word of the Lord brought forth in the latter days, and perhaps especially the Book of Mormon. (2 Nephi 25:18-19, 21.)

Another association of the ensign with the marvelous work and wonder can be drawn from the First Vision. When the Father and the Son appeared to Joseph Smith in the sacred grove in 1820, Joseph was informed that he was to join none of the churches of his day because the professors of those sects drew near to the Lord with their lips, but their hearts were far from him. The Lord said: "They teach for doctrines the commandments of men, having a form of godliness, but they deny the power thereof." (JS–H 1:19.) This is a quotation from the prophecies of Isaiah (Isaiah 29:13)—the wording is only slightly different. The prophecy continues with the Lord promising "to do a marvelous work among this people, even a marvelous work and a wonder." (Isaiah 29:14.)

Five of the early revelations in the Doctrine and Covenants speak of this marvelous work "about to come forth." (See D&C 4:1; 6:1; 11:1; 12:1; 14:1.) These revelations also show the Book of Mormon as a major part of the fulfillment of the promise of a marvelous work made to Nephi and foretold by Isaiah. Four of those five revelations continue with an admonition to give heed to the Lord's word (especially the Book of Mormon), and they also give directions to those who help bring it forth, then and later.[5] The initial ensign is clearly the Book of Mormon's coming forth as a marvelous work and a wonder among men.

Further analysis of the promise to Nephi and Lehi (2 Nephi 29:2) shows the Lord's designation of the time period for the coming forth of this marvelous work as the time he would set his hand the second time to recover his people, which are of the house of Israel. This is again a quotation from Isaiah. (See Isaiah 11:11.) In Isaiah, this quotation fits between two verses that both speak of an ensign being raised (verses 10 and 12). Furthermore, these same words that the Lord spoke to Nephi are found in Isaiah and are quoted twice more in the Book of Mormon. This further verifies that this ensign is the coming forth of the Book of Mormon, a marvelous work to be done in these latter days. (See 2 Nephi 25:17; Jacob 6:2.)

The Doctrine and Covenants also substantiates the important role of the Book of Mormon in becoming an ensign to the nations. The Lord commanded Joseph Smith to "pretend to no other gift" until the Book of Mormon translation was finished. (D&C 5:4.) Following a warning to those who will not hearken to his word (especially the Book of Mormon) that Joseph Smith would shortly be ordained to deliver unto the children of men, the Lord declared to the Prophet: "This generation shall have my word through you." (D&C 5:10.) In that context, "word" refers mainly to the Book of Mormon. This is substantiated when the Lord continues by promising to furnish additional witnesses to the work of bringing forth the Book of Mormon. (D&C 5:11-12.) In a later revelation, the Lord declared that after all these witnesses, the world would be judged, "even as many as shall hereafter come to a knowledge of this work." (D&C 20:13.)

The role of the Book of Mormon as a standard, or an ensign, for judging the world is also confirmed in the Book of Mormon itself. The Lord promised Nephi that the things Nephi wrote would be handed down from one generation to another as long as the earth should stand, and that "the nations who shall possess them shall be judged of them according to the words which are written." (2 Nephi 25:21-22.) These scriptures verify that the Book of Mormon is the Lord's word, an ensign, to our generation.

The importance of the Book of Mormon as an ensign was further emphasized in revelations to Hyrum Smith and David Whitmer. Hyrum was instructed to wait a little longer to preach until he had the Lord's word (the Book of Mormon) and the Lord's gospel (contained therein) and was thus sure in his doctrine. He was further told to study the Lord's word "which shall come forth among the children of men, or that which is now translating, yea, until you have obtained all which I shall grant unto the children of men in this generation." (D&C 11:15-16, 21-22.) David Whitmer was also told that the Lord would bring forth the fulness of the gospel (contained in the Book of Mormon) from the Gentiles to the house of Israel. (D&C 14:10.) The Lord continually reminded the people of the importance of the coming forth of the Book of Mormon as an ensign.

In June 1829, Joseph Smith completed the translation, and the Lord revealed to Oliver Cowdery, David Whitmer, and Martin Harris, the three special witnesses of the Book of Mormon, that the translation of the Book of Mormon was true. (D&C 17:6.)[6] The wording of the Lord's declaration ("as your Lord and your God liveth . . .") is one of the most solemn of oaths and is therefore a firm endorsement of the correctness of the translation. In the same month, the Lord again[7] reminded Oliver Cowdery that his work as a scribe during the translation had brought him many manifestations by the Spirit that the things he had written were true. The Lord commanded him to "rely upon the things which are written; for in them are all things written concerning the foundation of my church, my gospel, and my rock." (D&C 18:2-4.)

Many prophecies of Isaiah are quoted in the Book of Mormon. These quotations were taken from the plates of brass that were brought from Jerusalem. (1 Nephi 5:11-14.) Later Nephi was shown in vision that many plain and precious things would be lost from the original text of the Bible. A comparison of the Isaiah quotations in the Book of Mormon with the present-day biblical text of Isaiah verifies part of this loss. The Book of Mormon thus retains many important words, phrases, and prophecies that have been lost from the biblical text, which further shows its role as an ensign.

One of these Isaiah prophecies affirms the truth of the Book of Mormon translation.[8] After foretelling that some of the words of the Book of the Nephites would be delivered to the learned, who would reject them, Isaiah said that the book would be delivered again to the unlearned (Joseph Smith); for the Lord was able to do his own work. He declared through Isaiah: "Wherefore thou [Joseph Smith] shalt read the words which I shall give unto thee." (2 Nephi 27:20.) The translation of the words by the unlearned Joseph Smith was, of course, accomplished through the urim and thummim by the gift and power of God, and Oliver's work as scribe was to write the words as Joseph read them.[9] The Lord confirmed that Oliver had done his job well.

The Lord again gave testimony of the Book of Mormon in a revelation to Martin Harris. He commanded Martin to give financial support "to the printing of the Book of Mormon, which contains the truth and the word of God." He said that this ensign was his word to the Gentile, and that soon it would "go to the Jew, of whom the Lamanites are a remnant, that they may believe the gospel, and not look for a Messiah to come who has already come." (D&C 19:26-27.) Thus the Book of Mormon was translated and ready to be printed, and the marvelous work foretold by Isaiah was beginning to roll forth.

After the Book of Mormon was printed, the Lord was ready to organize his Church again upon the earth. The Church was organized on April 6, 1830, for which occasion the Lord revealed the importance of the Book of Mormon to the Church, as recorded in section 20 of the Doctrine and Covenants. He again declared that Joseph had been prepared and given power to translate and bring forth the book (D&C 20:5-8); that it was a record of a fallen people containing the fulness of the gospel to the Gentiles and the Jews (D&C 20:9); that it was substantiated by the ministering of angels to others who were to declare their witness to the world (D&C 20:10); that it proved to the world that the existing scriptures (the Bible) were true and that God was still calling people to his work in this generation as well as in generations of old (D&C 20:11); and that it showed the world that Jesus Christ was the same God yesterday, today, and forever (D&C 20:12). This last purpose verifies that the Book of Mormon is another testament of Jesus Christ.

Following a declaration of the role of the book in bringing people either to condemnation or to a crown of eternal life (D&C 20:13-16), the Lord revealed a lengthy list of doctrinal concepts reestablished by the Book of Mormon. These concepts range from the existence of God to the sanctification of his children. (D&C 20:17-36.) Thus the Book of Mormon became a doctrinal ensign to the newborn church.

After the Church was organized, the Lord periodically reminded the members of the role of the Book of Mormon. In August 1830, he referred to his having sent Moroni "to reveal the Book of Mormon, containing the fullness of [his] everlasting gospel," and to Moroni's having "the keys of the record of the stick of Ephraim." (D&C 27:5.) The reference to the record of the stick of Ephraim confirmed another Old Testament prophecy related to the coming forth of the Book of Mormon. (See Ezekiel 37:15-20.) Two months later, in October 1830, the Lord reminded two missionaries that the Book of Mormon as well as the holy scriptures (the Bible) were "given of [him] for [their] instruction; and the power of [his] Spirit quickeneth all things." (D&C 33:16.) Thus the Book of Mormon was to be an ensign in their missionary work as directed by the Holy Ghost.

Another three months passed, and the Lord, as he had promised (D&C 28:32), revealed his law to the Church (D&C 42). The law actually consisted of several laws. One of these was the law of teaching. About that law, the Lord commanded: "The elders, priests, and teachers of this church shall teach the principles of my gospel, which are in the Bible and the Book of Mormon, in the which is the fulness of the gospel." (D&C 42:12.) The Lord obviously did not want his Church to lose sight of the Book of Mormon as a teaching ensign.

When members of the Church realize that the Doctrine and Covenants confirms the revelations of the Old Testament prophets, especially Isaiah, which revelations the Savior said would be fulfilled when the covenants made to the house of Israel began to be fulfilled (3 Nephi 20:11-12), and that the prophecies of Nephi are being fulfilled in our day, then they will realize that an ensign has been raised to the nations, and that they are the bearers of that ensign.

The Book of Mormon is thus an ensign to bring the nations to Christ and his Church and to judge the world. It is also an ensign to the Church, to help Church members understand the Bible, to teach them correct doctrine, and to guide them in teaching and in missionary work.

2

A Choice Seer Brings
Forth the Ensign

The man who was to bring forth the Book of Mormon as a marvelous work in the latter days was foreordained of God (JS–H 1:33) and foreknown by many of the ancient prophets.[1] Most of the prophecies about this foreordained prophet, seer, and revelator have unfortunately been lost because of plain and precious parts that have been taken from the record of the Jews (See 1 Nephi 13:23-29) or concealed in the language of the scriptures so that only those who are spiritually attuned will recognize the correct interpretations of the passages. Fortunately, because the Nephite prophets had the plates of brass, the Book of Mormon restores some of the knowledge originally recorded by the Old Testament prophets. Nephi recorded upon his plates a covenant the Lord made with Joseph who was sold into Egypt; Lehi quoted this covenant to his sons. The covenant stated that in the last days the Lord would raise up a choice seer from the fruit of Joseph's loins, a seer who would do a great work among the house of Israel. (2 Nephi 3:4-7.)

Isaiah is another prophet who knew of this latter-day Joseph. He stands as an example of those prophets who wrote of Joseph in the veiled language of the scriptures. Yet, Nephi said, Isaiah's words are plain unto "all those that are filled with the spirit of prophecy." (2 Nephi 25:4.) Joseph of Egypt and Isaiah did know about Joseph Smith. While other prophets also knew about him, only some of the references of these two will be considered here.

The Prophecy of Joseph of Egypt

As recorded in the Book of Mormon, there are nine descriptions of the choice seer in Joseph's prophecy. All of these pointedly fit the prophet Joseph Smith, thus confirming him to be the seer spoken of by the Lord to Joseph of Egypt. In the first description, the Lord declared to Joseph: "A choice seer will I raise up out of the fruit of thy loins; and he shall be esteemed highly among the fruit of thy loins." (2 Nephi 3:7.) The fruit of Joseph's loins is divided into two major groups today—those who were scattered among the nations of the Gentiles with others of the house of Israel but have now been gathered into the Church (see D&C 86:8-10), and the group known to the members of the Church as the Lamanites, and to others as the American Indians. Both of these groups have confirmed their reverence for Joseph Smith, the seed of Joseph of Egypt.

Typical of the esteem many early members of the Church held for Joseph Smith is the testimony of Brigham Young, Joseph's successor as president of the Church:

> I honor and revere the name of Joseph Smith. I delight to hear it; I love it. I love his doctrine. What I have received from the Lord, I have received by Joseph Smith; he was the instrument made use of. If I drop him, I must drop these principles; they have not been revealed, declared, or explained by any other man since the days of the Apostles. If I lay down the Book of Mormon, I shall have to deny that Joseph is a Prophet; and if I lay down the doctrine and cease to preach the gathering of Israel and the building up of Zion, I must lay down the Bible; and, consequently, I might as well go home as undertake to preach without these three items.
>
> I feel like shouting Hallelujah, all the time, when I think that I ever knew Joseph Smith, the Prophet whom the Lord raised up and ordained, and to whom he gave keys and power to build up the kingdom of God on earth and sustain it.[2]

After Joseph Smith's martyrdom, Elder John Taylor wrote: "Joseph Smith, the Prophet and Seer of the Lord, has done more, save Jesus only, for the salvation of men in this world, than any other man that ever lived in it." (D&C 135:3.) Such accolades as these, representative of thousands of others, have led some to accuse the Latter-day Saints of worshiping Joseph Smith. To that accusation the Church answers an emphatic *no*—we do not worship him, but we reverence him as we do Moses, Abraham, and other of God's prophets. This reverence given to Joseph Smith certainly fulfills the prophetic words of the Lord to Joseph of Egypt: "He shall be esteemed highly among the fruit of thy loins." (2 Nephi 3:7.)

The esteem of Joseph Smith among the Lamanites, a major group of descendants of Joseph of Egypt, was not widespread early because Joseph Smith did not have a lot of association with them. However, the following incident shows how the Lord was working with the Lamanites to acquaint them with the prophet Joseph Smith so they would receive instructions from him.

> The Indian Chiefs remained at Nauvoo until the Prophet returned and had his trial. During their stay they had a talk with Hyrum Smith in the basement of the Nauvoo House. Wilford Woodruff and some others were present. They were not free to talk, and did not wish to communicate their feelings until they could see the great Prophet.
>
> At length, on the 2nd day of July, 1843, President Joseph Smith and several of the Twelve met those chiefs in the courtroom, with about twenty of the elders. The following is a synopsis of the conversation which took place as given by the interpreter: The Indian orator arose and asked the Prophet if the men who were present were all his friends. Answer—"Yes."
>
> He then said, "We as a people have long been distressed and oppressed. We have been driven from our lands many times. We have been wasted away by wars, until there are but few of us left. The white man has hated us and shed our blood, until it has appeared as though there would soon be no Indians left. We have talked with the Great Spirit, and the Great Spirit has talked with us. We have asked the Great Spirit to save us and let us live; and the Great Spirit has told us that he had

raised up a great Prophet, chief, and friend, who would do us great good and tell us what to do; and the Great Spirit has told us that you are the man (pointing to the Prophet Joseph). We have now come a great way to see you, and hear your words, and to have you to tell us what to do. Our horses have become poor traveling, and we are hungry. We will now wait and hear your word."

The Spirit of God rested upon the Lamanites, especially the orator. Joseph was much affected and shed tears. He arose and said unto them, "I have heard your words. They are true. The Great Spirit has told you the truth. I am your friend and brother, and I wish to do you good. Your fathers were once a great people. They worshiped the Great Spirit. The Great Spirit did them good. He was their friend; but they left the Great Spirit, and would not hear his words or keep them. The Great Spirit left them, and they began to kill one another, and they have been poor and afflicted until now.

"The Great Spirit has given me a book, and told me that you will soon be blessed again. The Great Spirit will soon begin to talk with you and your children. This is the Book which your fathers made. I wrote upon it (showing them the Book of Mormon). This tells what you will have to do. I now want you to begin to pray to the Great Spirit. I want you to make peace with one another, and do not kill any more Indians; it is not good. Do not kill white men; it is not good; but ask the Great Spirit for what you want, and it will not be long before the Great Spirit will bless you, and you will cultivate the earth and build good houses like white men. We will give you something to eat and to take home with you."

When the Prophet's words were interpreted to the chiefs, they all said it was good. The chief asked, "How many moons would it be before the Great Spirit would bless them?" He (Joseph) told them, not a great many.

At the close of the interview, Joseph had an ox killed for them, and they were furnished with some more horses, and they went home satisfied and contented.[3]

Certainly Joseph Smith brought both scattered Joseph and the Lamanites, groups of the fruit of the loins of Joseph of Egypt to a knowledge of the covenants the Lord had made with their fathers. (2 Nephi 3:7.)

He Shall Do None Other Work

In the second description of the choice seer, the Lord told Joseph of Egypt: "I will give unto him a commandment that he shall do none other work, save the work which I shall command him. And I will make him great in mine eyes; for he shall do my work." (2 Nephi 3:8.) Joseph Smith was commanded by the Lord to devote all his service to Zion, and he was promised that he would be given strength and the Lord would be with him. In temporal labors he was not to have strength, for this was not his calling. His calling was "to expound all scriptures, and continue in laying on of the hands and confirming the churches." (D&C 24:7-9.)

That Joseph Smith became great in the eyes of the Lord is shown by revelations the Lord gave concerning him. The Lord revealed that the Church was to receive Joseph's word as if from the Lord's own mouth. (D&C 21:5.) He also declared that no one was appointed to receive commandments and revelations in his church except Joseph Smith. (D&C 28:2; see also 42:2-4.) The Lord further promised Joseph Smith: "The keys of this kingdom shall never be taken from you, while thou art in the world, neither in the world to come; Nevertheless, through you shall the oracles be given to another, yea, even unto the church." (D&C 90:3-4.) In this promise, Joseph is designated as the head of the dispensation of the fulness of time and is thus still doing the Lord's work beyond the veil. As Brigham Young said: "It is his mission to see that all the children of men in this last dispensation are saved, that can be, through the redemption. . . . He was foreordained in eternity to preside over this last dispensation."[4]

He Shall Be Great Like Unto Moses

A third description of this choice latter-day seer was that he "shall be great like unto Moses." (2 Nephi 3:9.) There are many comparisons of these two great prophets.

As the president of the high priesthood, presiding over the whole church, Joseph Smith was "to be like unto Moses." (D&C 107:91.) Both Moses and Joseph Smith saw God face to face. (Moses 1:1-3; JS–H 1:17.) Both were called to do a specific work

for God. (Moses 1:6; JS–H 1:33.) Moses restored the knowledge
of God to his people, as did Joseph Smith. (Moses 1:31-32; D&C
130:22.) Moses had a vision to prepare him to write Genesis, and
the same vision was opened to Joseph Smith to prepare him to
translate Genesis as he revised the Bible. (Moses 1.) The list
could go on, but these few are sufficient to establish the parallel
between the two prophets.

He Shall Have Power to
Bring Forth the Lord's Word

The fourth description of this choice seer of the latter days
was that he was to be given power to bring forth the word of the
Lord to the seed of Joseph of Egypt. (2 Nephi 3:11.) This, of
course, refers to the Book of Mormon.

Joseph of Egypt's prophecy included the pronouncement that
this seer and the word of the Lord he would bring forth would also
convince Joseph's seed of the word of the Lord "which shall already have gone forth among them." (2 Nephi 3:11.) The Lord
revealed to Joseph Smith that one of the primary purposes of the
Book of Mormon was to prove "to the world that the holy scriptures [the Bible] are true." (D&C 20:11.) This shows again that
this description of the seer is the prophet Joseph Smith.

Joseph was further told by the Lord: "The fruit of thy loins
shall write; and the fruit of the loins of Judah shall write; and that
which shall be written by the fruit of thy loins, and also that
which shall be written by the fruit of the loins of Judah, shall grow
together, unto the confounding of false doctrines and laying down
of contentions, and establishing peace among the fruit of thy
loins, and bringing them to the knowledge of their fathers in the
latter days, and also the knowledge of my covenants." (2 Nephi
3:12.)

Joseph of Egypt's prophecy is similar to Ezekiel's famous
prophecy of the two sticks. Ezekiel may have based the wording of
his prophecy on Joseph's original prophecy, since it was recorded
in the brass plates. As time passes, this prophecy is being fulfilled
more and more as those who study the Bible and the Book of Mormon accomplish the objectives mentioned in the prophecy. The
work of Joseph Smith started all of this.

Out of Weakness He Shall Be Made Strong

In the fifth description of the choice seer, the Lord said: "Out of weakness he shall be made strong, in that day when my work shall commence among all my people, unto the restoring thee, O house of Israel." (2 Nephi 3:13.) This also is a fitting description of Joseph Smith.

Emma Smith in answer to a question asked by her son Joseph Smith III about whether or not his father could not have first written the Book of Mormon and then dictated it to the scribes, said: "Joseph Smith could neither write nor dictate a coherent and well worded letter, let alone dictating a book like the Book of Mormon, and though I was an active participant in the scenes that transpired, and was present during the translating of the plates, and had cognizance of things as they transpired, it is marvelous to me, 'a marvel and a wonder,' as much so as to anyone else."[5]

While this witness identifies a weakness Joseph Smith had at the beginning of his ministry, the growth and strength he gained through the blessings of the Lord are shown in sections 121, 122, and 123 of the Doctrine and Covenants. These three sections are excerpts from a letter he wrote while in jail at Liberty, Missouri, in March 1839. This letter was called by President Joseph Fielding Smith "one of the greatest letters that was ever penned by the hand of man."[6] It is really one of the great pieces of literature of this generation, especially when the conditions under which it was written are considered.

According to Oliver Cowdery, Joseph Smith's growth from weakness to spiritual strength also fulfills prophecy. Oliver said that the angel Moroni told Joseph Smith that this work would fulfill the scripture that says that "God has chosen the foolish things of the world to confound the things which are mighty."[7] This is a slight variation of 1 Corinthians 1:27. Joseph Smith certainly fulfilled this scripture as well as the prophetic declaration by Joseph of Egypt.

They That Seek to Destroy Him
Shall Be Confounded

The sixth characteristic of the latter-day choice seer was prophesied by Joseph of Egypt: "Behold, that seer will the Lord bless; and they that seek to destroy him shall be confounded." (2 Nephi 3:14.) This promise was reiterated to Joseph Smith in a revelation in December 1831, following the publication of some newspaper articles by Ezra Booth, who had apostatized. The revelation read: "If any man lift his voice against you he shall be confounded in mine own due time." (D&C 71:10.) Joseph's enemies were confounded many times as they attempted to stop the latter-day work.

On July 8, 1838, Joseph Smith received a revelation calling the Twelve on a mission to Great Britain. The revelation designated April 26, 1839, as their departure date from the temple site in Far West, Missouri. (D&C 118.) By the time this date arrived, it was unsafe for Mormons to be in Missouri, having been driven from the state by an edict from the governor. The Prophet was in chains in prison in Liberty, Missouri, and his enemies vowed that this revelation would never be fulfilled. Nevertheless, a majority of the Twelve returned and met on the Far West Temple site and fulfilled the conditions of the revelation. At the same time, the Prophet Joseph was liberated through the blessings of God.[8]

His Name Shall Be Called After Joseph

The seventh description of the choice seer was also prophesied by Joseph of Egypt: "His name shall be called after me; and it shall be after the name of his father." This, of course, fits Joseph, Jr., and his father, Joseph Smith, Sr. But the prophecy continues: "He shall be like unto me; for the thing, which the Lord shall bring forth by his hand, by the power of the Lord shall bring my people unto salvation." (2 Nephi 3:15.)

Just as Joseph had preserved the house of Israel in Egypt so his family could later return to their promised land, Joseph Smith brought forth the Book of Mormon, which has been the means of gathering millions of Joseph of Egypt's descendants out of the Gentile nations. As declared in the Doctrine and Covenants and confirmed by patriarchal blessings, these people are of the house of Israel, and particularly of Ephraim and Manasseh, the sons of Joseph.[9] They will eventually be given the land of America as promised to Joseph's seed. (Genesis 49:22-26; 3 Nephi 15:12-13.)

The eighth characteristic of the choice seer, according to the prophecy of Joseph of Egypt, again relates to Moses. Just as Moses had been given a spokesman (2 Nephi 3:17; Exodus 4:14-16), the Lord promised Joseph of Egypt a spokesman for the latter-day seer. The seer was to "write the writing of the fruit of [Joseph of Egypt's] loins," and the spokesman, also from the loins, was to declare it. (2 Nephi 3:18.) In October 1833, Sidney Rigdon was called by revelation to be the spokesman unto Joseph Smith. (D&C 100: 9-11.) Once more, the characteristic fits Joseph Smith.

The Words Shall Cry from the Dust

The ninth characteristic was declared by the Lord to Joseph of Egypt: "The words which he shall write shall be the words which are expedient in my wisdom should go forth unto the fruit of thy loins. And it shall be as if the fruit of thy loins had cried unto them from the dust." (2 Nephi 3:19.) This characteristic could be considered an extension of either the fourth or the eighth one, since they both deal with the writing of the fruit of the loins of Joseph of Egypt. Because it deals more with the message of those writings, it will be considered as a separate characteristic.

The words the seer was to write are obviously the Book of Mormon. This is consistent with Isaiah's prophecy, particularly as it is retained in the Book of Mormon, wherein the words of those who had slumbered (the Nephites, part of the fruit of Joseph's loins) would be delivered to this wicked generation, but the sealed portion of the plates was reserved for a future time. (See 2 Nephi 27:8-9; Isaiah 29; D&C 5:4-10.) The Lord further told Joseph of Egypt that these words (the Book of Mormon) would "cry from the dust; yea, even repentance unto their brethren, even after many generations have gone by them." (2 Nephi 3:20.) This is also a part of Isaiah's prophecy (see Isaiah 29:1-4), and Joseph's words are another witness of the Book of Mormon coming out of the ground. Its coming forth certainly fulfills the words of both Joseph of Egypt and Isaiah.

Conclusion of the Prophecy

The prophecy of Joseph of Egypt clearly designates Joseph Smith as the choice seer of the latter days. There is no other person in these latter days to whom any of the above descriptions

could apply. They all apply to Joseph Smith. As Nephi said of
Joseph of Egypt: "He truly prophesied concerning all his seed.
And the prophecies which he wrote, there are not many greater."
(2 Nephi 4:2.) More significant is the fact that those prophecies
were and are being fulfilled today through the work of Joseph
Smith and his successors in the Church he established.

Isaiah's Prophecies of Joseph Smith

When the angel Moroni appeared to Joseph Smith on September 22, 1823, "he quoted the eleventh chapter of Isaiah, saying that it was about to be fulfilled." (JS–H 1:40.) Although there
are many references in Isaiah to Joseph Smith, only chapter 11
will be treated herein. [10]

Isaiah chapter 11 is obviously a dual prophecy. Nephi and
Joseph Smith both interpreted it to be a prophecy about Christ (2
Nephi 30:8-10; D&C 113:1-2), but a careful analysis in light of
Moroni's declaration to Joseph Smith and D&C 113 shows it to
be also a prophecy of Joseph Smith.

The rod to come forth from the Stem of Jesse is identified by
the Lord through Joseph Smith as "a servant in the hands of
Christ, who is partly a descendant of Jesse as well as of Ephraim,
or of the house of Joseph, on whom is laid much power." (D&C
113:4.) The Lord revealed to Joseph Smith that he was a descendant of Joseph. He further revealed that the promises given to
Abraham were extended to Joseph because he was of the lineage
of Abraham and was therefore to do the work of Abraham. (D&C
132:30-32.) [11] Joseph Smith's patriarchal blessing, given by his
father, verifies his lineage from Abraham, and from Joseph and
Ephraim. [12] That his lineage is also from Jesse or Judah is not positively supported from other sources, but the revelation in Doctrine and Covenants section 113 sufficiently establishes it.

Furthermore, the Lord gave Joseph Smith "power from on
high, by the means which were before prepared, to translate the
Book of Mormon." (D&C 20:8.) This was the only power or gift
granted him until he finished the work of translation. (D&C 5:4.)
The two characteristics of the servant specified by the Lord, the
lineage and the power given him, definitely applied to Joseph
Smith.

The branch that was to grow out of his roots has reference to the church established by Joseph Smith. That the Book of Mormon was vital to the early Church is evident from a study of the early sections of the Doctrine and Covenants, as discussed in chapter 1. This is further supported by the New Testament.[13]

"The Spirit of the Lord resting upon him" in Isaiah 11:2-4 may have reference to Christ, as indicated in D&C 113, or to Joseph Smith as the servant in the hands of Christ. Certainly Joseph Smith had "the spirit of wisdom and understanding" upon him as he translated the Book of Mormon.

The Book of Mormon also was to judge the world. Nephi foretold that his words would be handed down "from generation to generation . . . according to the will and pleasure of God; and the nations who shall possess them shall be judged of them according to the words which are written." (2 Nephi 25:22.) This is in keeping with the spirit of John the Revelator's declaration that the angel who brought the book forth was to send it to every nation, kindred, tongue, and people with an adominition to fear God, for the hour of his judgment was come. (Revelation 14:6-7.)

The Lord further declared that this generation was to have the word of the Lord through Joseph Smith. (D&C 5:5-10.) The word of the Lord in this context is the end product of the translation of the Book of Mormon, Joseph's only gift at that time. Joseph was to disseminate the Book of Mormon to the world.

The eleventh chapter of Isaiah also prophesies of a servant who "shall stand for an ensign of the people; to it shall the Gentiles seek; and his rest shall be glorious." (Isaiah 11:10.) The Lord identified this servant as a literal descendant of Jesse (and therefore Judah) and Joseph "unto whom rightly belongs the priesthood, and the keys of the kingdom, for an ensign, and for the gathering of [God's] people in the last days." (D&C 113:6.) Some feel this is a different person than the servant in Isaiah 11:1 because, they reason, the Lord wouldn't speak of the same person two separate times but would have combined the two references into the same context. However, the Doctrine and Covenants also identifies this person as Joseph Smith.

The reason for his being mentioned twice is that the scripture is speaking of Joseph in two different roles. The lineage again fits.

Joseph Smith was a descendant of Abraham (D&C 132:30-32) to whom the priesthood rightfully belonged. The keys of the kingdom were committed to him. (See D&C 27:6-9, 12-13; 65:2; 90:2-4; 110:13-16; 128:20-21.) The ensign[14] refers to the church that would be organized after the Book of Mormon was translated. The Gentiles were to seek this ensign, which is clearly identified in the Doctrine and Covenants as the Lord's "everlasting covenant" that he had sent into the world. (D&C 45:9.) The everlasting covenant is later identified as the gospel. (D&C 133:57; see also D&C 1:22; 22:1.) Joseph Smith brought forth the Book of Mormon, which contains the fulness of the gospel (JS–H 1:41; D&C 20:9), and organized the Church, both being ensigns to the nations. This seems to leave no question regarding whom Isaiah is speaking about.

Without going into a detailed analysis of the rest of Isaiah 11, it speaks of these ensigns, the Book of Mormon and the Church, as bringing other nations into the everlasting covenant, and of Joseph Smith's role in fulfilling the covenant made to Abraham.

Verse 11 outlines the bringing in of the fulness of the gospel.[15] Verses 12 and 13 speak of the gospel's being taken to the various groups of the house of Israel, and verse 14 describes the inhabitants of the entire land given to Abraham, from the Euphrates to the river in Egypt (Genesis 15:18), being offered the gospel and coming under one dominion. Many of these are also Abraham's descendants. Verses 15 and 16 speak of the Lord's involvement in fulfilling the covenant to the house of Israel. Moroni quoted these verses to Joseph Smith in September 1823, saying they needed to occur to fulfill the gathering of Israel.[16]

Isaiah, Joseph of Egypt, and many other Old Testament prophets saw the mission of Joseph Smith in the latter days. He is the "choice seer," the literal seed of Joseph of Egypt, of whom they prophesied. The Lord's work was begun by his translating of the Book of Mormon and organizing the Church as ensigns to the nations. This work is still being carried out by his successors. The recipients of his great work should rejoice in the knowledge of his being foreknown and raised up to bring forth the Book of Mormon, a marvelous work and a wonder, and to establish the Church in the latter days.

3

The Scattering and
Gathering of Israel

The scattering and gathering of Israel is a prevalent theme in the Old Testament.[1] While nearly all of the prophets testified about one or more aspects of this scattering and gathering, only one of them, to our knowledge, foretold the whole prophetic picture. The writings of this prophet, Zenos, were apparently once part of the Old Testament, as they were recorded on the brass plates; but they were probably lost from the Bible when plain and precious parts were removed from it. (1 Nephi 13:23-29.)[2] This whole prophetic picture, given in the form of an allegory, is available today because Jacob recorded it on the small plates he received from Nephi. Today this allegory can be read in the Book of Mormon in the fifth chapter of Jacob. It gives an understanding of the sequence of the gathering of Israel, which was initiated by the coming forth of the Book of Mormon, an ensign for gathering the nations of Israel.

The fifth chapter of Jacob is one of the most challenging in the Book of Mormon. Although it is the longest chapter in the book, the analysis and interpretation of the chapter, not its length, present the challenge. The interpretation is difficult because the elements of the story stand for something outside the story. In this way, the allegory and the parable are similar. Both illustrate a principle under the guise of another story, but the allegory is longer and more involved. The apostles asked Jesus why he taught in parables. He answered, "Because it is given unto you to know the mysteries of the kingdom of heaven, but to them it is not given." (Matthew 13:11.) According to Joseph Smith, the disciples of Jesus were able to receive the correct interpretation, but the unbelievers were not.[3] These unbelievers could be divided into two categories: those who were not yet ready to receive the truth, and those who had hardened their hearts against it. Therefore, a parable rewards the faithful, is an act of mercy to those who are not yet spiritually attuned, and is a condemnation to those who reject the spirit of truth. (See Matthew 13:10-17.)

The importance and difficulty of the Allegory of the Olive Tree were noted by President Joesph Fielding Smith: "In this chapter we have a parable[4] that nobody could have written unless he had the guidance of the Spirit of the Lord. It would have been impossible. I think that as many as ninety-nine out of every hundred who read the Book of Mormon read this parable through without grasping the fulness and meaning of it. And I think this is one of the greatest passages in the Book of Mormon."[5]

To understand the allegory, it is helpful to see the setting in which Jacob quotes it. After apologizing for not being able to write many of his words because of the difficulty of engraving upon plates (Jacob 4:1), Jacob bears testimony of the Nephites' knowledge of Jesus Christ (Jacob 4:4-9). Following some personal admonitions to the reader (Jacob 4:10-13), Jacob prophesies that the Jews will "reject the stone upon which they might build and have safe foundation" (Jacob 4:15). He continues his prophecy by declaring that the scriptures teach that "this stone shall become the great, and the last, and the only sure foundation, upon which the Jews can build." (Jacob 4:16.)[6] To support his thesis, he quotes the allegory. (Jacob 5.)

Imagery of the Allegory

Before analyzing the allegory, it is essential to understand its imagery (what each of the figures in the allegory represents). The allegory itself identifies most of the imagery. Those images not identified by the allegory can be identified from other scriptural sources or from latter-day prophets (see table 1 at the end of the chapter).

The tame olive tree represents the house of Israel. (Jacob 5:3.) The wild olive tree is identified as the Gentiles by the apostle Paul, in writing to the Romans. (Romans 11:13-17.) From these sources, we can determine that the branches of the tame olive tree are the various tribes of the house of Israel: the lost ten tribes, the nation of Judah, and the Nephite-Lamanite groups of the tribe of Joseph. The branches of the wild olive tree are the various Gentile nations. The roots represent the blood of Israel. This interpretation is based on the following statement of President Joseph Fielding Smith and an overall analysis of the allegory as supported by other scriptures: "In brief, it [the allegory] records the history of Israel down through the ages, the scattering of the tribes to all parts of the earth; *their mingling with, or being grafted in, the wild olive trees, or in other words the mixing of the blood of Israel among the Gentiles* by which the great blessings and promises of the Lord to Abraham are fulfilled."[7] (Italics added.)

As taught by Lehi, grafting refers to the receiving of the fulness of the gospel or to coming to a knowledge of the true Messiah. (1 Nephi 10:14; 15:13-16.)

That the vineyard represents the world is shown by comparing Jacob 5:77 with Jacob's comment that the world will be burned with fire after it is pruned the last time. (Jacob 6:2-3.)

The master of the vineyard is Jesus Christ. This is shown in the Doctrine and Covenants where the revelator refers to the last time that he shall call laborers into his vineyard (D&C 33:3) and then identifies himself in various ways. The revelator refers to the church he has established. (D&C 33:5.) This church is The Church of Jesus Christ of Latter-day Saints. He says further that he will gather his elect. (D&C 33:6.) A comparison with Matthew 23:37 also identifies the revelator as Jesus Christ. The revelator next identifies the principles of his gospel. (D&C 33:11-12.) A comparison with 3 Nephi 27:13-22 again confirms the revelator to be Jesus Christ. Jesus Christ then speaks of the coming of the Bridegroom, saying that he will come quickly (D&C 33:17-18), which, compared with Matthew 25:1 and Revelation

22:20 once more shows the speaker to be the Savior. This is consistent with the Savior's New Testament teaching: "One is your master, even Christ." (Matthew 23:8-10.)

The last figure we need to identify is the servant. Servants collectively are identified by Amos as the prophets. (Amos 3:7.) The main servant who comes to the vineyard with the Lord of the vineyard could be a specific prophet or a representation of the prophets generally. Or, the servant may be the head of each dispensation, such as Joseph Smith, who holds the keys of this dispensation. (D&C 90:2-4.) However, the interpretation of just which prophet the servant is does not affect the message of the allegory as long as it is kept in mind that the servant of the allegory is a prophet.

Through this imagery, one can see that the allegory teaches the history, scattering, and gathering of the house of Israel. This can best be understood by referring to other related scriptures. (See table 2 at the end of this chapter.)

Analysis of the Allegory

Since the allegory outlines the history of the scattering and gathering of the house of Israel, it is only logical that it starts at the beginning. The house of Israel began about 1800 B.C., when the twelve sons of Jacob were living in Canaan. The allegory ends when the temporal existence of the earth is completed, or, in other words, at the end of the millennium.

A careful analysis of the allegory shows that it refers to seven time periods (see table 3 at the end of the chapter). Two of these time periods are described as merely a long time between the visits of the Lord and his servant to the vineyard. (Jacob 5:14, 29.) These seem easily identified. The first would be the end of the prophets, about four hundred years before the advent of the promised Messiah, a period when no revelation was given to Israel. The second would be the great apostasy following the Savior's ministry until the day of the restoration, another period when no revelation was given to Israel. The identification of the other five time periods is made easier by identifying these two. The five are (1) from Jacob to Malachi, the last of the Old Testament prophets; (2) the ministry of Jesus Christ; (3) the restoration in 1820 to the millennium; (4) the millennium; and (5) the end of the earth.

The Scattering of Israel

The first period covers from about 1800–400 B.C. This is the time that Israel was scattered "upon all the face of the earth, and also among all nations." (1 Nephi 22:3.) The interpretation of Jacob 5:3-14 is drawn from the scriptures and history of this time.

Jacob 5:3-6. After introducing the allegory (Jacob 5:1-2), Jacob begins quoting it. The house of Israel is described as a tame olive tree that is waxing old and beginning to decay. Because of this condition, the Lord of the vineyard pruned it, nourished it, and digged about it in an attempt to save it. (Jacob 5:3-5.) This attempt could be identified as the time when the house of Israel was in Egypt, because of the famine in Canaan. (Genesis 39-50.) The famine in all the land (Genesis 41:56-57) is indicative of the decaying of Israel. God does use famine and drought to bring his people to repentance so that he might bless them. (Helaman 12:2-3.) While some may argue that this is a transplant rather than a pruning because Jacob (Israel) had left Canaan (the promised land) and sojourned in Egypt, it should be remembered that the land covenanted to Abraham, and thus the house of Israel, extended "from the river of Egypt unto the great river, the river Euphrates." (Genesis 15:18.) Therefore, the house of Israel is still in the main part of the vineyard. Furthermore, the biblical account of Genesis supports the pruning concept. Joseph tells his brothers that God had sent him to preserve them and that he should *nourish* them in Egypt for five years. (Genesis 45:5, 7-8, 11; 46:1-7.)

The allegory continues with the observation or prophecy "that after many days it began to put forth somewhat a little, young and tender branches; but behold, the main top thereof began to perish." (Jacob 5:6.) The phrase "after many days" fits the extended time Israel was in Egypt, from the time of Joseph until their bondage in the days of Moses. The young and tender branches have a double interpretation.

First, when Moses led Israel out of Egypt, the Lord became angry with the people because they would not hearken to His voice after having seen His glory and the miracles He did in Egypt. They were therefore detained in the wilderness for forty years until the older generation, except Joshua and Caleb, died (the main top perished) and the new faithful generation (the young and tender branches) were allowed to enter Canaan. (Numbers 14:26-38.)

Second, Moses sought diligently to prepare his people to behold the face of God through the ordinances and power of the Melchizedek Priesthood. But Israel hardened its heart, and God took the Melchizedek Priesthood (the main top) out of their midst and left the lesser or Aaronic Priesthood (the young and tender branches) to prepare the new generation for future opportunities. (D&C 84:19-26.) The Lord had worked with Israel, but Israel had failed to respond to his efforts.

Jacob 5:7-14. The next program of the Lord of the vineyard was to graft some wild branches (Gentiles) into the tame olive tree and to graft many of the young and tender branches whithersoever he would. (Jacob 5:7-9.) The main branches are different from the main top, which had earlier begun to perish. The main branches are possibly the two divisions of the kingdom of Israel—the northern tribes (Ephraim) and the southern tribes (Judah). Both of these branches were plucked off because of their wickedness—Israel in about 721 B.C. by the Assyrians, and Judah about 589 B.C. by the Babylonians. Many people from both branches were destroyed, which is the equivalent of the burning referred to in the allegory. Those who destroyed them also took away the young and tender branches.

One of the grafts into the tame olive tree can be identified as the Gentiles that Assyria brought to intermarry with the Israelites who had been left behind after the Assyrian conquest. (Isaiah 7:17-18; 2 Kings 17:18-23; 18:9-11.) The Gentiles' exposure to the roots of the house of Israel is shown by Israelite priests later being sent to teach them how to worship the God of Israel. (2 Kings 17:24-28.) God does work in mysterious ways.

Another Gentile graft into the tame olive tree would be the Babylonian captivity of Judah, in which many of Judah were carried into Babylon, as prophesied by Jeremiah. (Jeremiah 25:8-11.) We do have an account of some of Judah intermarrying with Gentiles at this time. (Ezra 2:61; Nehemiah 7:61-64.) This graft's productivity was furthered through the work of the Gentile King Cyrus of Persia, an instrument in the hands of God (Isaiah 44:28–45:4), as well as the prophets of exile, Ezekiel and Daniel.

A further grafting may have taken place as Jeremiah and many of the Jews went down into Egypt after the Babylonian captivity. (Jeremiah 43.) We have no account of this, but the same pattern probably applies.

While the Gentiles were grafted into Israel, many of the Israelites were also scattered among the Gentiles. This accounts for the roots of Israel being identified as yet alive among the Gentiles. (Jacob 5:54.) This preservation of the roots is the purpose for the grafting as given in the allegory. (Jacob 5:11.) It also fulfills the prophecy of Amos that the Lord would "not utterly destroy the house of Jacob" but would sift them "among all nations, like as corn is sifted in a sieve." (Amos 9:8-9.) This was also foretold by Nephi, based on Isaiah's prophecies. (1 Nephi 22:3.)

While Israel was scattered among the nations, three groups (Jacob 5:39) or branches were kept intact but planted elsewhere in the vineyard. These can be identified in the order in which they were taken away: the ten tribes (about 721 B.C.), the Jews (about 607 B.C.), and the Lamanites about (600 B.C.). Keeping this order in mind is very important in understanding later parts of the allegory.

Thus, the first period of the allegory is from about 1800–400 B.C., when the house of Israel was "scattered upon all the face of the earth, and also among all nations." (1 Nephi 22:3.) The second period is one of apostasy, from 400 B.C. to the ministry of Jesus Christ. It is covered in one verse (verse 29) and needs no further commentary.

The Earthly Ministry of Jesus

The third period describes the ministry of Jesus and the apostles in the meridian of time, as is outlined in Jacob 5:16-28. This is the period of which all the Old Testament prophets had spoken. (Mosiah 14:33-34.)

Jacob 5:16-18. The first observation about this period in the allegory is that the Gentile branches that had been grafted into the tame olive tree were bearing good fruit. (Jacob 5:16-18.) One place where this part of the allegory was fulfilled is the city of Samaria, where the Savior, at a well originally dug by Jacob, asked a Samaritan woman for a drink of water. The Samaritans were the product of the intermarriage between the Israelites who remained in the land after the Assyrian conquest of 721 B.C. They married the Babylonians and other Gentiles brought in by the Assyrians. (2 Kings 17:24.) Taking advantage of his disciples' amazement that he was conversing with the Samaritan woman, Jesus taught them that the field of the Samaritans was ready for the gospel harvest. (John 4:31-42.) The graft had taken hold, and the mixture of the Israelites and Gentiles was bearing fruit.

While there are no other definite accounts in the scriptures of the Gentile graft bearing fruit, there is another possibility to be considered. Who were the wise men who came from the east to herald the birth of the King of the Jews? (Matthew 2:1-2.) Could these possibly have been a product of the Jewish and Babylonian graft stemming from the Nebuchadnezzar captivity of 607 B.C.? It is certainly a possibility.

Jacob 5:19-28. The second event of this period is when the Lord of the vineyard and his servant visited the natural branches that had been grafted into the nethermost parts of the earth. (Jacob 5:19.) Their first visit was to the first branch that had been taken away. This would be the ten and a half tribes that had been taken into Assyria and then led further into the north. (2 Kings 18:9-12.) While we do not know their location, we do know they were visited by the Savior after his resurrection and his appearance to the Nephites. (3 Nephi 16:1-4.)

The branch was producing much good fruit. The servant questioned the Lord about his having brought this branch to what was the poorest spot of ground in the vineyard. The Lord responded that the servant should not give counsel, for he [the Lord] knew it was a poor spot, but the branch had produced fruit. The Lord knows all things and guides his children to accomplish his purposes.

As further evidence of his wisdom, the Lord invites the servant to look at a branch that had been planted in an even poorer spot of ground. It too had brought forth much fruit. (Jacob 5:23.) This undoubtedly refers to the Jews, but whether it is a group in Babylon, Egypt (the Coptics), or those restored in Palestine is not clear.

The Lord next invites the servant to behold the third branch that had brought forth fruit. (Jacob 5:24.) Some interpret this branch as different from the one described in verse 25; however, a comparison with verse 39 shows there are only three branches. This is also supported historically, since the Savior mentioned only three groups of Israelites that he had visited or would yet visit. (3 Nephi 15-17.) Verses 25 through 28 are, therefore, an extension of the description of the third group. That they had been planted in a choice spot of ground (Jacob 5:25) helps to identify them as the people of Lehi in America. (1 Nephi 2:20.) Further verification of their being the seed of Lehi (and Ishmael) is shown by the allegory's declaration that only a part had brought forth tame fruit while the other part had brought forth wild fruit. (Jacob 5:26.) This, of course, represents the division of Lehi's people into Nephites and Lamanites. (2 Nephi 5:5-25.) The nourishing and pruning mentioned in the next three verses (2 Nephi 5:26-28) must refer to the period between A.D. 34 and 36, when all were converted to the Lord. (4 Nephi 1-2.) Their work was productive for a time.

The Restoration of the Covenant of Israel

The fourth period is the apostasy after Jesus' ministry. The fifth period has the longest treatise of any period (Jacob 5:30-75), which is logical since it depicts the fulfillment in the latter days of the covenant made to Israel. It was to precede the time when "the end soon cometh" (Jacob 5:29), the Second Coming of Christ. This is substantiated by the angel Moroni's visit to Joseph Smith in September 1823, as Moroni recited many passages of scripture about the coming of Christ with the admonition that they were not yet fulfilled but soon would be. (JS–H 1:36-41.)

Jacob 5:30-37. The first eight verses (30-37) of this period of the allegory describe the visit of the Lord of the vineyard and his servant to the Gentiles who had been grafted into the house of Israel. This is easily interpreted by comparing it to Joseph Smith's history as recorded in the Pearl of Great Price. "All sorts of fruit which did cumber the tree" fits the description Joseph Smith gave of the religions revivals that were prevalent in his youth; many religions claimed to be the true religion. (JS–H 1:5-9.) The Lord's tasting of all the fruit with the declaration that none of it was good corresponds with what we call the First Vision. In response to Joseph's question about "which of all the sects was right," the Savior told him to "join none of them, for they were all wrong." (JS–H 1:18-19.) The servant's observation that the wild branches had "nourished the roots, that they are alive" can be understood by referring to the Doctrine and Covenants explanation of the servant of the Lord referred to in Isaiah chapter 11. The servant (Joseph Smith) is identified as "a descendant of Jesse, as well as of Joseph." (D&C 113:3-6.) Thus Joseph Smith had the literal blood of Israel in his veins although he was living among the Gentiles and was by culture a Gentile. The blood of Israel had been scattered among the Gentiles and by some genetic process had been preserved. Although this may not be proven scientifically, it is a truth fully supported by the Old Testament prophets.[8] This is further verified in the Doctrine and Covenants.[9]

Jacob 5:38-50. After the Lord and his servant visited the Gentile grafts, they went to the natural branches that had been planted in the nethermost parts of the vineyard. All of these had become corrupt, including the wild fruit (Lamanites) that overcame the tame fruit (Nephites), whose branch withered away and died. (Jacob 5:38-40.) The fall of the Nephites is recorded in Mormon 6:10-15. The wild fruit that remained (Lamanites) is described in Mormon 5:15-16.

The Lord lamented over the loss of the natural branch he had planted "in a good spot of the ground." The land was, he emphasized, "choice unto me above all other parts of the land of my vineyard." (Jacob 5:43.) Those he had cut down so that he "might plant this tree" (Jacob 5:44) were the Jaredites (Omni 20-21; Ether 13:20-21).

In answer to the Lord's query of what he could have done more, the servant suggested that the branches had overcome the roots and had taken strength unto themselves. (Jacob 5:47-48.)

This probably describes the appointment of officers in the church and kingdom. As apostasy crept in, the apostles and other stalwart officers were killed or imprisoned. Others were given these positions, but their appointments were not by revelation. They were appointed by political officers rather than church officers. This is best exemplified under the rule of Constantine, where Christianity was made the state religion and the priesthood offices were filled by the emperor's appointment rather than by the Lord through his prophets and apostles. The Lord's suggestion that they should cut down the vineyard and burn it and the servant's plea to spare it a little longer (Jacob 5:49-50) display the laws of justice and mercy. Justice would rule that the vineyard be destroyed, but mercy pleads to appease justice. (Alma 42:15.)

Jacob 5:51-60. Having yielded to mercy, the Lord presents his plan to save his vineyard. It is outlined in verses 52 through 54 and is implemented in verses 55 and 56. These verses must be carefully studied. The Lord's plan is to graft the natural branches of Israel back into the tree from which they had been taken. The mother tree into which the Gentile branches had been grafted was to have these branches (which produce the most bitter fruit) removed so the natural ones could be grafted in their stead. The roots of the natural branches would then be preserved. (Jacob 5:52-53.) The Israelite roots of the Gentile branches were yet alive; therefore, the Lord would establish these Gentile branches as a mother tree into which he could graft the natural branches when the mother tree was sufficiently strong to sustain that graft. (Jacob 5:54.) This was done, and then the natural branches were grafted back in. (Jacob 5:55-56.) This is the overall plan.

The first step—the establishment of the mother tree, as father Lehi had explained—was to come through the fulness of the Gentiles, or in the latter days when the fulness of the gospel would come unto the Gentiles and from them to scattered Israel. (1 Nephi 10:14; 15:12-14.) In other words, the Church would have to be established among the Gentiles before it could bring back the natural branches. The house of Israel had been scattered among the Gentiles, and the roots were still alive (the blood of Israel was still among the Gentiles). The mother tree must be reestablished as a tree of Israel, by the gospel being preached to the

Gentiles, and by those of the blood of Israel (roots) becoming the tree.

It is only logical as well as scriptural that the mother tree be established through the birthright holder of the house of Israel, Ephraim. Jeremiah foresaw this movement and described it. (Jeremiah 31:1-9.) Also, the Lord has confirmed by revelation that the early priesthood holders of the Church were "lawful heirs, according to the flesh." (D&C 86:8-9.) President Joseph F. Smith made this observation in 1902: "A striking peculiarity of the Saints gathered from all parts of the earth is that they are almost universally of the blood of Ephraim."[10]

The Lord further prescribed that the pruning be light, cutting off only the most bitter wild branches, until the natural branches could derive nourishment from the natural roots or true vine. (Jacob 5:57-60; 1 Nephi 15:15-16.) The true vine is identified as Jesus Christ in John 15:1. He, of course, is the source of strength to his covenant people who are grafted back or have come to the knowledge of the true Messiah. (1 Nephi 10:14.)

Jacob 5:61-74. Having outlined the program, the Lord instructs his servant to call servants to prune the vineyard for the last time. (Jacob 5:61-62.) Jacob's interpretation of the allegory was that when the Lord "set his hand again the second time to recover the remnant of his people" (Isaiah 11:11), it would be the last time that he would nourish and prune his vineyard and then the end would soon come. (Jacob 6:2.) That this is the work of the restoration is confirmed in modern-day revelation. In October 1830, the Lord called Ezra Thayer and Northrop Sweet to prune his vineyard for the last time. (D&C 33:3-4.) The Book of Mormon, the initial ensign, was to be a primary instrument in that pruning. (D&C 33:16.) Therefore, that nourishing and pruning began over a hundred and fifty years ago and is well under way. Ephraim is firmly established, and the time to begin grafting back the natural branches is near.

The grafting of the natural branches is to be in the reverse order of their dispersion. The last taken away (Lehi's group) is to be the first grafted back. (Jacob 5:63-64.) The work of the Lamanites has commenced. The second group to be planted in the nethermost part of the vineyard (Judah) is also being prepared.

The last branch, the lost tribes, have not yet been positively identified but will be grafted back in the Lord's own due time.

After these natural branches have been grafted back and begin to grow, the Lord gives further instructions about their pruning. The pruning is to be carefully done according to the strength of the good branches. The roots and the top are to be kept equal in strength. (Jacob 5:65-69.) These instructions correspond with those given in the Doctrine and Covenants. Just as the vineyard is to be leniently pruned, the Church is to find favor with the people of the world until Israel becomes great and is sanctified. (D&C 105:26-31.) Furthermore, before the Lord comes in wrath upon the earth, the Church is to be cleansed or pruned. (D&C 112:23-26.)

As the servant of the Lord calls other servants, although they are few, they are promised joy as they lay up fruit unto the Lord. (Jacob 5:70-71.) This is much like the Lord's admonition to Oliver Cowdery and David Whitmer to remember the worth of souls and the joy they would receive in bringing one or more souls to Christ. (D&C 18:10-16.) The allegory continues with the work of the servants progressing until the trees become "like unto one body; and the fruits were equal." (Jacob 5:74.) This is the same concept taught by Ezekiel in the uniting of the tribes of Israel under one shepherd. (Ezekiel 37:15-23.)

Jacob 5:76-77. The allegory concludes with two verses covering two periods of time. The first (Jacob 5:76) describes the millennium, wherein the Lord will lay up fruit for a long time (one thousand years). The second is the end of the millennium, when evil fruit will again appear and the Lord will gather both the good and the bad together, preserving the good and casting away the bad. Following this, the vineyard will be burned. (Jacob 5:77.) The temporal existence of the earth will then be completed and the program of the house of Israel finished.

Jacob's Interpretation

Jacob's commentary on the allegory (Jacob 6) is brief but appropriate. After bearing testimony of the surety that the allegory will be fulfilled, he speaks of the blessedness of the servants of the Lord and the mercy of God in remembering the house of Israel, both the roots (those scattered among the Gentiles) and the branches (those planted in the nethermost parts of his vineyard). He concluded with personal admonitions to the reader.

Following a general plea for repentance (Jacob 6:5-7), Jacob poses some thought-provoking questions. (Jacob 6:8.)

The first question, "Will ye reject these words?" refers to the allegory. (Jacob 6:8.) Remember that this allegory was written probably long before 600 B.C. It has been fulfilled exactly as foretold through the first four periods and it is well into the fifth. That the remainder of it will be fulfilled is certain; therefore, we should not reject the allegory.

The second question is, "Will ye reject the words of the prophets?" Zenos is not the only prophet who has foretold the destiny of Israel. Every aspect of the allegory can be supported or supplemented by other prophets.

The third question, "Will ye reject all the words which have been spoken concerning Christ, after so many have spoken concerning him?" is another affirmation that all the prophets have testified of Christ. (Jacob 4:4-5; 7:11.) Jacob then enumerates other ways we can learn the truth about Christ—by Christ's own word, by receiving the gift of the Holy Ghost, and by the witness of the Holy Spirit. Those who reject these sources mock the great plan of the redemption of Israel and will be brought to stand "with shame and awful guilt before the bar of God." (Jacob 6:9.)

Finally, Jacob returns to his plea to repent and be wise by entering the strait gate (baptism) and continuing in the narrow way until eternal life is obtained. Jacob then bids us farewell until he meets us at the pleasing bar of God, which bar strikes the wicked with awful fear and dread. (Jacob 6:11-13.)

The Lord is over all the earth. He is in charge and will bring about his purposes. Our challenge is to be wise and to follow his program as directed by his servants the prophets.

Table 1:
IMAGERY OF THE ALLEGORY

The tame olive tree = the house of Israel. (Jacob 5:3; 1 Nephi 10:12; 15:12.)
The wild olive tree = the Gentiles. (Romans 11:11-25.)
The roots of the olive tree = the blood of Israel among the Gentiles.
          (Joseph Fielding Smith, *Answers to Gospel Questions* 4:141.)
Grafting = receiving the fulness of the gospel or coming to a knowledge of the
          true Messiah. (1 Nephi 10:14; 15:13-16.)
The vineyard = the world. (Jacob 5:77; 6:2-3.)
Master of the vineyard = Jesus Christ. (D&C 33; Matthew 23:8-10, 37; 25:1;
          Revelation 22:20; 3 Nephi 27:13-21.)
The servant = the prophet or prophets. (Amos 3:7; Joseph Smith, *Teachings of the Prophet Joseph Smith*, p. 157.)

Table 2:
INTERPRETATIONS FROM THE SCRIPTURES

Verses from Jacob 5		Compare
1-2	Introduction	Romans 11:13-26
3-5	Israel decays	Genesis 41:56-57; 45:1-11; 46:1-7
6	Main top	D&C 84:19-26; Numbers 14:26-38
7-11	Wild branches	2 Kings 17:18-24 (Assyria); 2 Kings 24:14 (Babylon); Isaiah 44:28–45:4 (Cyrus)
8-14	Young, tender branches	2 Kings 18:9-12 (lost tribes); Genesis 49:22-26; Jeremiah 28:8-10 (Judah); 2 Nephi 3:5; 10:20 (Lehi)
16	Jesus' ministry	Mosiah 14:33-34
17-18	Gentile graft	John 4:31-42; Matthew 2:1
19-22	Lost tribes	3 Nephi 16:1-4
23	Jews	Acts 20:21
24-28	People of Nephi	3 Nephi 15:21-24
29	The end soon cometh	JS–H 1:36-41
30-32	All sorts of fruit	JS–H 1:5-9, 19
33-37	Roots are alive	D&C 113:5-6; 86:8-10; 103:17
38-40	All corrupt	Mormon 5:15-16; 6:10-15
41-43	A choice land	Ether 2:12
44-45	Cumbered the land	Omni 20-22; Ether 13:20-21
46-48	Roots overcome	Matthew 15:1-9; Isaiah 24:5-6
49-51	Spare the vineyard	Alma 42:15; Exodus 32:7-14
52-56	Mother tree	1 Nephi 10:14; 15:12-14; D&C 86:8-11; Jeremiah 31:1-9
57-60	Trees pruned	John 15:1-8
61-62	The last time	D&C 33:3-4; 39:17; Jacob 6:2
63-64	The last shall be first	Matthew 20:1-6; 3 Nephi 21:22-28
65-69	Branches pruned	D&C 105:26-31; 112:23-26
70-71	The servant's joy	D&C 18:10-16
72-74	One body	Ezekiel 37:15-23
75	Servants called	D&C 116; Daniel 7:13-14, 22
76	A long time	D&C 45:58; Revelation 20:3-6
77	The earth burned	Revelation 20:7-9

Table 3:
The Seven Time Periods of the Allegory

Verses 3-14. From Jacob to the end of the prophets. About 1800-400 B.C.	Verse 15. A long time passed away.	Verses 16-28. The Ministry of Jesus Christ. About A.D. 30-34	Verse 29. A long time passed away.	Verses 30-75. The Restoration, about A.D. 1820 to the Millennium.	Verse 76. A long time passed away.	Verse 77. The end of the earth.
A. Verses 3-5. The nourishing of the decaying olive tree—the house of Israel (Israel in Egypt). B. Verse 6. The main top begins to perish (the wilderness). C. Verse 7. The grafting in of the wild olive branches (Gentiles; Assyria, Babylon, etc.). D. Verses 8, 12-14. The grafting of the natural branches into the nethermost parts of the vineyard (dispersion of Israel). 1. Lost Tribes. 2. Jews. 3. Nephites and Lamanites. 4. People among all nations.	The end of the prophets to the ministry of Jesus Christ, about 400 B.C. to A.D. 30.	A. Verses 16-18. The visit to the Gentile grafts—the Samaritans, etc. B. Verses 19-28. The visit to the natural branches of Israel. 1. The first (lost tribes) had produced good fruit. 2. The second (Jews) had produced good fruit. 3. The last had produced tame fruit (Nephites) and wild fruit (Lamanites).	From the apostasy following the ministry of Jesus Christ and His apostles to the restoration of the gospel through Joseph Smith, about A.D. 1820.	A. Verses 30-37. The visit to the wild-branch grafts (the Gentiles). No fruit is good, but the roots are alive. B. Verses 38-48. The visit to the natural branches of Israel, all corrupt. C. Verses 49-75. The grafting back of Israel into the mother trunk. 1. The roots (blood of Israel among the Gentiles) preserved. 2. The natural branches grafted back—the last to be first. a. Lamanites. b. Jews. c. Lost Tribes.	The Millennium, 1,000 years.	A. The good and bad gathered together. The good preserved, the bad cast out. B. The vineyard burned with fire.

4

An Ensign to the Scattered Remnant of Ephraim

Jacob, the brother of Nephi, labored diligently to record the lengthy allegory of the olive tree in spite of the difficulty of engraving upon plates. He did this to assure the permanency of this important document. (Jacob 4:1.) Some of his commentary following the allegory is needed to analyze the role of Ephraim, the holder of the birthright of the house of Israel and the bearer of the Book of Mormon as an ensign to other nations.

Jacob first identified the time of the last pruning of the Lord's vineyard, the house of Israel, as the period when the Lord would "set his hand again the second time to recover his people . . . and after that the end soon cometh." (Jacob 6:2.)

"The end soon cometh" is obviously a reference to "the end of the world, or the destruction of the wicked" at the time of the Lord's Second Coming. (JST Matthew 1:4.) This is further substantiated in Jacob's commentary when he notes that the world will be burned by fire. (Jacob 6:3.)

The reference to a second recovery of the Lord's people is similar to the statement from Isaiah 11:11, which chapter was quoted to Joseph Smith in September 1823 by Moroni, who said that "it was about to be fulfilled." (JS–H 1:40.) The second recovery of Israel was also foretold by Jeremiah as a time of gathering, not from Egypt, but "from the land of the north, and from all the

lands whither he had driven [Israel]." (See Jeremiah 16:14-16.)
Thus Jacob and Moroni both interpret Isaiah's prophecy as refer-
ring to a latter-day gathering prior to the Second Coming, and
Jeremiah's prophecy verifies this concept of a latter-day gathering.

Jacob continued his commentary by acknowledging the
mercy of God because "he remembereth the house of Israel, both
roots and branches." (Jacob 6:4.) His statement is appreciated
more when one identifies the branches and the roots.

The three branches of the natural tree, or the house of Israel,
spoken of in the allegory are easily identified as the lost tribes, the
tribe of Judah, and the Lamanites.

The roots of Israel are not as easily identified. According to
the Bible, the roots must primarily represent Ephraim, or at least
the tribe that was to be gathered out first to establish the mother
tree and bear the ensign to the world. This conclusion seems valid
because Ephraim holds the birthright. (Jeremiah 31:9.) Thus,
Ephraim headed the ten tribes.

The name *Ephraim* was often used to designate the entire nation of the ten northern tribes. (See Isaiah 7:2; 11:13.) At least
some of these ten tribes were scattered among the nations of the
earth (Amos 9:8-9), but they were promised that a remnant
would return. (Isaiah 6:13; 10:20-22, 27.) Considering the patriarchal blessings given to the Latter-day Saints who have been
gathered, Ephraim seems to have been the dominant tribe that
was scattered, and the remnant is now being gathered. The Book
of Mormon teaches much about this scattering and gathering and
about Israel's work after they are gathered. An analysis of the
Book of Mormon teachings shows that it is truly an ensign to scattered Israel, especially Ephraim.

Scattered Among the Nations

In commenting on Isaiah's writings, Nephi told Laman and
Lemuel "that the house of Israel, sooner or later, [would] be scattered upon all the face of the earth, *and also among all nations.*" (1
Nephi 22:3; italics added.) Understanding of this scattering en-
ables us to better comprehend the Savior's teachings to the
Nephites about the words of Isaiah. He taught that Isaiah "spake
as touching all things concerning [Christ's] people which are of

the house of Israel; therefore it must needs be that he must speak also to the Gentiles." (3 Nephi 23:2.) Note that the Savior did not say that Isaiah spoke *about* the Gentiles, but that he was to speak "*to* the Gentiles." The reason Isaiah (through his writings) was to speak to the Gentiles is that the house of Israel was scattered among them. If Isaiah were to speak *all things* concerning the house of Israel to them, he could not do so unless he spoke to the Gentiles among whom they were scattered. This is further confirmed by a subsequent verse in which the Savior declares that the words he was speaking to the Nephites should be written; then, "according to the time and the will of the Father," they would "go forth unto the Gentiles." (3 Nephi 23:4.)

Undoubtedly, the Father wanted his Son's words to go to the Gentiles to gather the remnant of Israel, particularly Ephraim, from among them. The time when the Father would bring about this gathering is also spoken of in the Book of Mormon.

The Gathering of the Remnant

After speaking of the plates he had made with his own hands, of recording the events he had seen with his own eyes, and of the blessings of Jesus Christ to him and to the children of Lehi, Mormon prophesied that Jesus Christ would "again bring a remnant of the seed of Joseph to the knowledge of the Lord their God." (3 Nephi 5:23.) This confirms the earlier declaration that Ephraim was to be gathered first.

Ephraim is the son of Joseph and succeeded him in the birthright. It is also evident that this prophecy was fulfilled through the First Vision. (See JS–H 1:7-20.) Joseph Smith was a descendant of Joseph, son of Jacob, through the loins of Ephraim. This was made known to the Prophet as the Lord explained Isaiah's writings. (See Isaiah 11; D&C 113.) The Lord confirmed not only Joseph Smith's lineage, but also the promise that to him rightly belonged "the priesthood, and the keys of the kingdom, for an *ensign*, and for the *gathering of my people* in the last days." (D&C 113:3-6; italics added.) The ensign, again, is the Book of Mormon and the Church, both of which the Prophet Joseph would bring forth.

Certainly Joseph Smith, as a literal descendant of Ephraim

and of Joseph who was sold into Egypt to preserve Israel, was foreordained to translate the Book of Mormon as an ensign to gather Israel in the latter days and to preserve them from the destruction at the second coming. All of this began when Joseph Smith obtained a correct knowledge of God in the First Vision, as had been foretold by the Nephite prophet Mormon. (3 Nephi 5:23.)

In the First Vision, Joseph beheld "two Personages, whose brightness and glory defy all description," standing above him in the air. One of them spoke to him, calling him by name and said, pointing to the other, *"This is My Beloved Son. Hear Him!"* (JS–H 1:17.) This vision taught Joseph that the trinitarian concept of God is incorrect. He learned that the Father and the Son were separate and distinct personages, and he later observed that they had bodies "of flesh and bones as tangible as man's." (D&C 130:22.)

Before the vision of the Father and the Son, Joseph's tongue was bound by an evil power, and thick darkness surrounded him. But Joseph called on God in his heart and mind, and the darkness was replaced by a pillar of light. (JS–H 1:15-16.) This experience naturally taught Joseph much about God and about the powers of Satan. He learned that God lives and answers prayers, and that the divine influence is greater than the power of Satan. It was this knowledge that he brought to other descendants of Ephraim as he fulfilled the work of establishing the ensigns, the Book of Mormon and the Church.

Mormon also foretold the continuation of the great work of the Lord in gathering Israel that was begun by Joseph Smith. "As surely as the Lord liveth, will he gather in from the four quarters of the earth all the remnant of the seed of Jacob, who are scattered abroad upon all the face of the earth." (3 Nephi 5:24.)

Joseph Smith's calling to gather the remnant of Israel was confirmed by a visitation of Moses on April 3, 1836. Moses committed to him "the keys of the gathering of Israel from the four parts of earth, and the leading of the ten tribes from the land of the north." (D&C 110:11.) Note that the keys are divided into two parts: the gathering from the four parts of the earth, which would include those scattered among the Gentiles (the roots of the allegory); and the leading of the ten tribes from the north, or the restoration of this branch spoken of in the allegory of the olive tree.

Joseph Smith began the work of gathering Jacob. While he still holds the keys of the last dispensation, through him the keys were passed on to The Church of Jesus Christ of Latter-day Saints (D&C 90:3-4), which Church has continued to lift the Book of Mormon as an ensign to the nations and gathered many more of Ephraim, the remnant of Jacob.

Mormon also prophesied of the gathering of the other branches of Israel that were scattered upon all the face of the earth. (1 Nephi 22:3.) He wrote: "As [God] hath covenanted with all the house of Jacob, even so shall the covenant wherewith he hath covenanted with the house of Jacob be fulfilled in his own due time, unto the restoring all the house of Jacob unto the knowledge of the covenant that he hath covenanted with them. And then shall they know their Redeemer, who is Jesus Christ, the Son of God; and then shall they be gathered in from the four quarters of the earth unto their own lands, from whence they have been dispersed; yea, as the Lord liveth so shall it be." (3 Nephi 5:25-26.)

Note the mention of a gathering from the four quarters of the earth in these verses, just as there was in verse 24. Just as Nephi made a distinction between the scattering of the house of Israel upon the face of the earth (the branches) and among all nations (the roots), Mormon seems to make a distinction between the gathering of the remnant (the roots that were scattered) and the restoring of the house of Jacob (the scattered branches) to their own lands.

The first group, Ephraim, was to come to a knowledge of the Lord, and the second group was to come to a knowledge of the covenant made to their fathers and to "know their Redeemer, who is Jesus Christ, the Son of God." (3 Nephi 5:26.) The true knowledge of God was restored through Joseph Smith, while the knowledge of Jesus Christ as the Son of God and Redeemer was to come to the house of Jacob as they were joined to Joseph's remnant Ephraim, those who had already been gathered and knew the truth about God.

Isaiah's Witness of the Remnant

Nephi quoted Isaiah as a third witness of Christ. (2 Nephi 11:2-3.) He also quoted him as another witness of "the covenants of the Lord which he hath made to our fathers." (2 Nephi 11:5.) The chapters he quoted refer frequently to the preservation of a remnant of Israel and depict the tribes of Israel as living among the Gentiles. The remnant may again be identified as Ephraim.

When Isaiah was called, the Lord said that his ministry was to continue until the cities were left without inhabitants and the Lord had removed the men far away. (Isaiah 6:11-12.) This undoubtedly refers to the destruction and taking away of northern Israel or the ten tribes in about 721 B.C.[1] The Lord then promised Isaiah that a tenth would return. (Isaiah 6:13; 2 Nephi 16:13.) In this prophecy, the Lord employed the symbol of a tiel-tree and an oak whose leaves were eaten, yet the holy seed was spread through their leaves. Importantly, this tenth could be interpreted to be either a percentage of all the people or one of the tribes. If the latter is the correct interpretation, the tribe would be Ephraim, the holder of the birthright. This would establish the allegory's mother trunk of the house of Israel, which was necessary to graft in the natural branches. Furthermore, the scattering of this holy seed (another implication of the birthright) would refer to Ephraim's being scattered among the Gentiles and Ephraim's subsequent return.

Through Isaiah, the Lord said that after northern Israel had been destroyed by the Assyrians, and after a great light had come to Galilee (the extended Galilean period of Christ's ministry), Assyria, which represents the Gentiles collectively, would also be punished for its failure to acknowledge the Lord's hand. (Isaiah 8-10; 2 Nephi 18-20.) Following these events, "the remnant of Israel, and such as are escaped of the house of Jacob, shall no more again stay [depend] upon him that smote them [the Gentiles], but shall stay upon the Lord, the Holy One of Israel, in truth." (Isaiah 10:20; 2 Nephi 20:20.)

The Lord further declared that "the remnant shall return, yea, even the remnant of Jacob, unto the mighty God." (Isaiah 10:21; 2 Nephi 20:21.) Returning to the mighty God is reminiscent of Mormon's prophecy of a remnant of Joseph or Ephraim coming to a knowledge of God. (3 Nephi 5:23.) Following the Lord's explanation of how he will bring this about, he declared to Israel "that his [the Gentile's] burden shall be taken away from off [Israel's] shoulder, and his [the Gentile's] yoke from off [Israel's] neck, and the yoke shall be destroyed because of the anointing [the covenant made to Abraham and thus Israel]." (Isaiah 10:27; 2 Nephi 20:27.) Note too that Isaiah chapter 11, which Moroni told Joseph Smith was soon to be fulfilled, is an explanation of how this covenant will be brought about. The prominence of the blood of Ephraim in the Church further substantiates the gathered remnant as Ephraim.

Many other passages in Isaiah confirm this concept besides the two quoted by Nephi. (See Isaiah 19:23-25; 27:12-13.) However, these two establish Isaiah as a third witness, with Nephi and Jacob (2 Nephi 6:5), that the house of Israel would be restored through Ephraim in the latter days. The purpose of that gathering is further amplified in the mission of scattered Israel as it is gathered.

The Mission of Scattered Israel

The reasons for the Lord's scattering Israel among the nations are made known to us through Isaiah as interpreted by Nephi and later by the Savior when he visited the Nephites. The primary reason was that scattered Israel was to be the servant of the Lord in gathering the rest of Israel.

Addressing those of Israel who had been scattered upon the isles of the sea, the Lord declared: "Thou art my servant, O Israel, in whom I will be glorified." (Isaiah 49:1-3; 1 Nephi 21:1-3.)[2] The Lord, through Isaiah, then outlined three aspects of the gathering: "It is a light thing that thou shouldest be my servant to raise up the tribes of Jacob, and to restore the preserved of Israel. I will also give thee for a light to the Gentiles, that thou mayest be my salvation unto the ends of the earth." (1 Nephi 21:6.)

The servant's mission was to raise up the tribes of Jacob. The tribes of Jacob are, of course, the twelve tribes of Israel.

These twelve tribes were separated into three groups as they were scattered upon the face of the earth. (Jacob 5:39.) The three groups were the lost tribes, the Jews, and the Lamanites. The scattering of the house of Israel among all nations had preserved the blood, or roots, of Israel. Israel's mission was also to restore the preserved of Israel. These were to be gathered from the Gentile nations. Through this gathering, scattered Israel's mission was further fulfilled. Not distinguishing between the Gentiles and those who were of the blood of Israel, the gospel was to be taken to all the Gentiles, and thus Israel was to be the bearer of the light or ensign, the Book of Mormon, to the Gentiles. Those who were not of the blood of Israel and accepted the gospel would be adopted into Israel. This would fulfill the covenant made to Abraham that through his seed should "all the families of the earth be blessed, even with the blessings of the Gospel." (Abraham 2:11.)

Naturally, the branches of Israel will constitute the majority of these three groups who will accept the gospel. (See Isaiah 54:1.) Therefore, the Lord probably listed them first rather than in the chronological order in which the gospel would be taken to them.

The chronological order is that the Book of Mormon, the ensign, would be taken to the Gentiles. This was to gather out the preserved of Israel (primarily Ephraim) from among the Gentiles. Simultaneously, Ephraim would bear the light to the Gentiles. This period is designated in the scriptures as "the times of the Gentiles." (D&C 45:28.) Following this period, the Book of Mormon was to go to the house of Israel, an event initiated as the Gentiles rejected the gospel that had come among them. This the scriptures call "the times of the Gentiles fulfilled." (D&C 45:30; Luke 21:24; 3 Nephi 16:10-12.)

Establishment of America

The preaching of the Book of Mormon to the Gentiles could not be brought to pass before the discovery of the Americas. A place where the ensign could be proclaimed freely needed to be established. The lands of America had been kept hidden for this very purpose. (2 Nephi 1:6-8.) According to the Savior's explanation to the Nephites, the Father first desired to establish the Gentiles in this land as a free people so that the Book of Mormon might be brought forth. (3 Nephi 21:1-4.) It could not be brought forth in Europe or other lands because state religions had been established. Nephi had foreseen that the Saints of God would be yoked with a yoke of iron and brought down into captivity. (1 Nephi 13:5.) Rome is known historically as the Iron Kingdom. In my opinion, this yoke was initiated with the establishment of a state religion under Constantine.[3]

While the major strength of the yoke was broken through the Protestant reformation, each nation set up its own state religion, thus maintaining circumstances that would deter the restoration of the gospel. God honors the agency of his children, and therefore, in his foreknowledge, had preserved the Americas to establish a free country where the Book of Mormon could be revealed and translated.

The Book of Mormon was to come forth as an ensign to the Gentiles and to go from the Gentiles as an ensign to the seed of the Nephites, whom the Savior had visited in the Americas. (3 Nephi 21:2, 5.) In a scriptural sense, "the Gentiles," who are to take the Book of Mormon to the Nephites, must be those who live in the Americas and thus are cultural Gentiles, although some are literally of the blood of Israel, the roots spoken of. (See 3 Nephi 16:6.) In the words of Elder Wilford Woodruff: "The Gospel is now restored to us Gentiles, for we are all Gentiles in a national capacity."[4]

Nephi also prophesied that this mighty Gentile nation would be raised up in the Americas. (1 Nephi 22:7.) The Savior said that this nation would become mighty because the Holy Ghost would be poured out upon it. In their might, he said, its people would smite the seed of Nephi and his brethren upon this land. (3 Nephi 20:27-28.) The nation's might was also to come through a divinely inspired constitution. (D&C 101:78-80; 98:5-8.) The men who established this divine document may also have been of the blood, or roots, of Israel. This suggestion arises from their appearance to President Wilford Woodruff in the St. George Temple in 1878 with an urgent plea:

> Two weeks before I left St. George, the spirits of the dead gathered around me, wanting to know why we did not redeem them. Said they, "You have had the use of the Endowment

House for a number of years, and yet nothing has ever been done for us. We laid the foundation of the government you now enjoy, and we never apostatized from it, but we remained true to it and were faithful to God." These were the signers of the Declaration of Independence, and they waited on me for two days and two nights. I thought it very singular, that notwithstanding so much work had been done, and yet nothing had been done for them. The thought never entered my heart, from the fact, I suppose, that heretofore our minds were reaching after our more immediate friends and relatives. I straightway went into the baptismal font and called upon brother McCallister to baptize me for the signers of the Declaration of Independence, and fifty other eminent men, making one hundred in all, including John Wesley, Columbus, and others; I then baptized him for every President of the United States, except three; and when their cause is just, somebody will do the work for them.[5]

Further evidence of their possible ties to the blood of Israel is shown in the fact that many leaders of the Church have established their ancestry through the lineage of these founding fathers:

Eight former presidents of the United States are among numerous famous people of the past and present who share ancestors with President Spencer W. Kimball. Intensive research by professional genealogists . . . has disclosed the different ancestral lines that link the Church leader with other well-known individuals in America.

Among the famous kin of President Kimball are former U.S. Presidents John Adams, a sixth cousin three times removed (6c3r); John Quincy Adams, (5c4r); Chester A. Arthur, (6c2r); Franklin Pierce, (1c2r); Grover Cleveland, (1c6r); Herbert Hoover, (6c1r); Richard M. Nixon, (8c); and Gerald R. Ford, (7c2r).

(If relatives are the same generation from a common ancestor, they are cousins. If they are one generation either up or down, they are once removed; if they are two generations either up or down, they are twice removed and so on).

Former U.S. vice presidents related to President Kimball are Hubert H. Humphrey, who was a double cousin, fifth and sixth, through two common ancestors; Nelson A. Rockefeller, (7c2r); and Aaron Burr, (1c2r), who killed Alexander Hamilton in a duel while serving as president.[6]

When the Book of Mormon would come to the seed of Nephi and his brethren, they were to know that the times of their promised blessings were near at hand. This was the sign promised to them by the Savior. (3 Nephi 21:1, 6-7.) They were told further that it would come in a day when the "kings [of the Gentiles would] shut their mouths." (3 Nephi 21:8.) Interestingly, while the strong Gentile nations had traditionally been ruled over by kings, when the Book of Mormon came forth, the kings had relinquished their political rule to parliaments and so had figuratively shut their mouths.

The Savior also prophesied of the work of his servant who would bring forth a marvelous work (the Book of Mormon) that most of the Gentiles would reject. (3 Nephi 21:9; see also D&C 45:29.)[7] He further interpreted Isaiah's words about the marring of the servant's visage. (3 Nephi 21:10.) He told the Nephites: "The life of my servant shall be in my hand; therefore they shall not hurt him, although he shall be marred because of them. Yet I will heal him, for I will show unto them that my wisdom is greater than the cunning of the devil." (3 Nephi 21:10.)

Speaking of the loss of the first 116 manuscript pages of the translation of the Book of Mormon, the Lord used the very words of his prophecy to the Nephites. He instructed Joseph to translate the remaining record of Nephi (the small plates) and not to retranslate that which was lost. The Lord declared: "I will not suffer that they shall destroy my work; yea, I will show unto them that my wisdom is greater than the cunning of the devil." (D&C 10:38-43.)

Following the raising of the ensign to the Gentiles, those who rejected it were to be cut off from the Lord's gathered remnant. (3 Nephi 21:11.) This rejection would lead the Gentiles to an internal conflict that would destroy many of them. (3 Nephi 21:12-20; 1 Nephi 22:13.) Those Gentiles who would accept the gospel, although few in number, would be privileged to help the gathered remnants of Joseph and others build a New Jerusalem upon the

American continent. (3 Nephi 21:21-23.) Following the building of the New Jerusalem, the natural branches of Israel are to be grafted back to the mother tree. (3 Nephi 21:24-28.)

Thus the remnant of Ephraim scattered among the Gentiles, or the roots, was to become the instrument of the Lord in initiating the final gathering of the house of Israel before the Second Coming. It would do this by proclaiming the Book of Mormon. Ephraim's work would be basically complete with the establishment of Zion, or the New Jerusalem, in the Americas. God, in his mercy and foreknowledge, had sent Ephraim to earth among the Gentiles to bring about his eternal purposes.

5

An Ensign to the Gentiles

When Jesus ministered among the Jews, he taught that the first would be last and the last would be first. (Matthew 19:30.) Jesus was teaching that after the Jews had rejected the gospel, the gospel would be taken to the Gentiles. Furthermore, he was teaching that in the latter-day restoration of the gospel, the Gentiles would be given the opportunity to accept the gospel first, and then it would be taken to the Jews and the other tribes of Israel. This interpretation is verified in the New Testament (Romans 2:9-10) and the Doctrine and Covenants (D&C 19:27; 90:8-9; 133:8) and is more specifically detailed in the Book of Mormon.

The term *Gentile* has many different definitions. The Savior gave this definition when he visited the Nephites: "Blessed are the Gentiles because of their belief in me, in and of the Holy Ghost, which witnesses unto them of me and of the Father." (3 Nephi 16:6.) The Gentiles, by this definition, are the Christian nations who believe in the Father, the Son, and the Holy Ghost. That this definition is correct can be shown by reviewing what the Lord taught during his Jerusalem ministry.

The Savior declared that he was "not sent but unto the lost sheep of the house of Israel." (Matthew 15:24.) He also instructed his apostles to "Go not into the way of the Gentiles." (Matthew 10:5.) During his ministry, he did not personally teach the Gentiles. Later, Peter received the revelation to take the gospel to the Gentiles. (Acts 10.) Therefore, the Gentiles (by this definition) are those nations that accepted Christ through the missionary efforts of Paul, the teacher of the Gentiles (1 Timothy 2:7; 2 Timothy 1:11), and other apostles. They are today basically the European nations or the Christian nations. Since the United States and Canada were settled primarily by Europeans, they, too, are Gentile nations.

The Covenant with Abraham

God promised Abraham that in him and in his seed "all families of the earth [would] be blessed." (Genesis 12:3; Abraham 2:11.) The Book of Mormon repeatedly refers to this promise. (1 Nephi 15:18; 22:9; 3 Nephi 20:25.) This blessing would undoubtedly come as his name became "great among all nations." (Abraham 2:9.) Although Abraham is reverenced among the Jews, the Moslems, and the Christians, many other nations do not yet know of him or the blessings that will follow their acceptance of the covenant that originated with him. The Book of Mormon prophets taught extensively how, when, and where these blessings will come, and it is through their teachings in the Book of Mormon that this blessing of Abraham will be fulfilled.

Lehi spoke much about the Gentiles, and Nephi commented on his remarks. (1 Nephi 10:11-14; 15:13-18.) Nephi saw a vision of the nations and kingdoms of the Gentiles, both in the meridian of time and in the last days. (1 Nephi 13-14.) Nephi and Jacob, commenting on the words of Isaiah, spoke of the Gentiles in the promised land of America. (1 Nephi 22:6-10; 2 Nephi 10:8-19; 26:12–30:3.) When the Savior appeared to the Nephites, he gave many prophecies about the Gentiles of the latter days. (3 Nephi 16:6-15; 20:15-20, 27-28; 21:2-24.) Mormon wrote to the Gentiles as he abridged the records of the Nephites (3 Nephi 30:1-2; Mormon 3:17; 5:9-10, 19-24), and Moroni wrote to them to whom the Book of Mormon would come forth (Ether 2:9-12; 4:6-13; 8:23-26; 12:22-41.) An analysis of all of these teaches how and when the ensign would be lifted to the Gentiles.

Gentiles in the Meridian of Time

The Book of Mormon speaks of the Gentiles in three different times. One of these is the meridian of times; the others are two separate yet continuous periods in the last days. These latter-day periods were designated by the Savior as the times of the Gentiles (D&C 45:28) and the fulness of the Gentiles, or the times of the Gentiles being fulfilled. (Luke 21:24; JST 21:32. See also Romans 11:25; JS–H 1:41.)

The events concerning the Gentiles in the meridian of time can be summarized in one historical movement. After the gospel was taken to the Gentiles by the apostles and the Holy Ghost bore witness of its truth, the great and abominable church was established among them. This organization was responsible for the loss of many plain and precious parts from the record of the Jews. Since the Book of Mormon is primarily written to the people of the latter days, not much more needs to be said about this event. However, it is necessary to understand that it did take place in order to see the significance of events among the Gentiles in the latter days, as foretold in the Book of Mormon. These events are now under way.

The Times of the Gentiles

The times of the Gentiles are when the Gentiles would have an opportunity to accept or reject the gospel, and thus the covenant of Abraham, in these last days. However, the Book of Mormon describes how God will have prepared the Gentiles for this opportunity before it is actually given. It records the Savior's teaching to the Nephites that all kindreds of the earth would be blessed in fulfillment of the covenant made to Abraham by "the pouring out of the Holy Ghost through [Christ] upon the Gentiles, which blessing upon the Gentiles shall make them mighty above all, unto the scattering of [Christ's] people." (3 Nephi 20:27.)

The blessings given the Gentiles would include discovering America, modern conveniences, and technology for the advancement of the human race. This advancement would make the Gentiles the ruling powers of the world, mighty in intellectual, social, and physical skills undreamed of in past years.[1] The spiritual dimension was to come through the restoration of the gospel. According to Mormon, all these blessings could have been enjoyed by the Nephites, but, since they fell away from Christ and followed Satan, the Lord reserved these blessings for the Gentiles. (Mormon 5:17-19.)

The first step in bringing the spiritual blessings to the Gentiles was to establish a free people in the Americas. To accomplish this, the Spirit of God wrought upon a man (Columbus) among the Gentiles (in Europe) and led him to the promised land (the Americas). Other Gentiles were also wrought upon by that Spirit to bring them out of the captivity to the promised land. (1 Nephi 13:13-14.)

What the captivity was is not explained in the Book of Mormon. I believe that it was a spiritual bondage brought about by state religions.

Nephi earlier saw the binding of the Saints with a yoke of iron, which brought them into captivity. As suggested in the previous chapter, the yoke of iron was the state religion of Rome established by Constantine. This yoke had been broken down through the reformation, but other yokes, or other state religions, still limited the freedom of religion in those countries. The Gentiles in Europe were thus in captivity to their political systems and could not exercise religious freedom. For this reason, God had preserved this land for the establishment of a free people (3 Nephi 21:4) and had kept it from the knowledge of other nations so that it would not be overrun and leave no place to establish a free people. (2 Nephi 1:8.)

As the Gentiles were established in the land, the Lord blessed them, and they prospered. (1 Nephi 13:15-16; 2 Nephi 10:10.) However, their mother Gentiles gathered together to battle against them. Again the Lord came to the aid of those Gentiles he had inspired to settle his choice land. His power was upon them, and his wrath was upon their mother Gentile enemies. Finally, the choice land was delivered out of their enemies' hands. (1 Nephi 13:17-19.) Nevertheless, in their blessed and prosperous condition, the Gentiles afflicted and scattered the house of Israel [the Lamanites]. (1 Nephi 13:14; 15:17; 2 Nephi 10:18; Mormon 5:20.)

However, the Lord would not allow the Gentiles to utterly destroy the seed of Nephi and his brethren, but he would bless the

Gentiles to establish a mighty nation in the promised land of America. This blessing would prepare for the restoration of the gospel. (1 Nephi 13:30-32; 22:7; 3 Nephi 20:28.) In their prosperous circumstances, the Gentiles were to become nursing fathers and mothers both temporally and spiritually to the Lamanites. (1 Nephi 14:6; 21:22-23; 22:6, 8-9; 2 Nephi 10:18.) This mighty Gentile nation was to be a land of freedom so that the Book of Mormon could be brought forth as an ensign to those Gentiles. (2 Nephi 10:11-16; 3 Nephi 21:4.)

The coming forth of the Book of Mormon was referred to as "a great and a marvelous work" by Nephi and by the Savior. (1 Nephi 14:5-8; 22:8-10; 3 Nephi 21:9-10.) This designation was undoubtedly because of the Lord's involvement in bringing it forth. One of its major purposes was to establish the truth of the Bible and restore plain and precious truths that had been lost. (1 Nephi 13:33-42.) Through this great and marvelous work, the fulness of the gospel would thus come to the Gentiles. (1 Nephi 15:7; 3 Nephi 16:7.)

The Book of Mormon prophets described the time when their work would come forth as an ensign to the Gentiles. Nephi interpreted Isaiah as foretelling the conditions that would exist and also the details of its coming forth. (2 Nephi 26:14–28:23.) Nephi also issued a warning to those who would reject the Book of Mormon. (2 Nephi 28:24-32.) Also, he foretold the reaction of the Gentiles to the Book of Mormon and gave admonitions in answer to those reactions. (2 Nephi 29.) Moroni likewise expressed concern over the Gentiles' reaction to this ensign and recorded the Lord's answer to his concerns. (Ether 12:22-41.)

In summary, those Gentiles (really Israelites scattered among the Gentiles) to whom this ensign was restored were responsible to take it and its gospel message to the other Gentiles throughout the earth. (1 Nephi 15:13; 2 Nephi 30:3; 3 Nephi 21:2-3, 5-7.) Thus, the other Gentiles have the opportunity to be numbered with the house of Israel and through adoption receive all the blessings of Abraham. (1 Nephi 14:1-2; 3 Nephi 30:13.) However, at the same time, the devil's work through the great and abominable church, will also spread throughout the earth. (1

Nephi 14:9-17.) This will cause the majority of the Gentiles to reject the gospel. Thus, the times of the Gentiles will come to a
close.

The Times of the Gentiles Fulfilled

Jesus taught his disciples about the generation in which the
times of the Gentiles would be fulfilled. (JST Luke 21:24-32.)
Another account of his teachings about this time was restored
through Joseph Smith in the Doctrine and Covenants section 45
(see verses 16, 24-30). While these sources tell us what will happen during this time, the Book of Mormon tells much more about
why they will happen. God the Father pronounced a woe upon
"the unbelieving of the Gentiles" who had been shown such great
mercies, and he commanded Jesus to tell the Nephites that when
the Gentiles sinned against the gospel and rejected its fulness, he
would take the fulness of the gospel from among them. In their
sins, they would be "lifted up in the pride of their hearts above all
nations, and above all the people of the whole earth, and . . . be
filled with all manner of lyings, and of deceits, and of mischiefs,
and all manner of hypocrisy, and murders, and priestcrafts, and
whoredoms, and of secret abominations." (3 Nephi 16:8-10.)
One does not have to step back very far to see that present-day society is guilty of all these sins.

Only the Father can measure the point at which the Gentiles'
pride will be greater than that of all nations. But when the Gentiles reject the fulness of the gospel, undoubtedly the missionaries
will be withdrawn from those nations, as described by Isaiah and
recorded by Nephi. Isaiah saw the missionaries carried away to
safety from a land and a people who would be roaring against
them, and only darkness and sorrow would be left in the land.
Isaiah further recorded that the light in the heavens would be
darkened because of these actions. (2 Nephi 15:29-30; Isaiah
5:29-30.) This could happen to one nation at a time and not to all
Gentile nations at once.

Also, these prophecies are probably conditional, based upon
the Gentiles' rejection of the ensign. (3 Nephi 21:14.) Those who
repent and accept the gospel will have the church established
among them. They will be numbered with the house of Israel and

will then be able to help build Zion and gather the rest of the children of Israel. (3 Nephi 21:21-24.) This gathering will follow the Gentiles' rejection of the gospel. (1 Nephi 10:14; 3 Nephi 16:11-13; 21:11.) However, those who reject the gospel will be trodden down by the house of Israel. (3 Nephi 16:14-15; 20:15-20; 21:12-21; Mormon 5:24.) This treading down was described by Micah and probably also by Isaiah. I draw this conclusion because the treading down is described in the Book of Mormon references referred to above in nearly identical terms to Micah's (4:12-13; 5:8-15), but the Savior refers to Isaiah as his source. [2]

The treading down by the house of Israel is not limited to the Lamanites; it will also be fulfilled by the Jews and perhaps others of the house of Israel. [3] It is also probable that this treading down will be done by the house of Israel before the gospel is preached to them; at least it will be done by those who have not yet had the gospel preached to them, as shown by the context and chronology of the Book of Mormon quotation. The sequence always has the Gentiles rejecting the gospel, then the Gentiles being trodden down by the Israelites, and finally Israel's hearing the gospel. This will happen at various times in different places.

The Message to the Gentiles

The most important message to the Gentiles is Nephi's admonition that "Jesus is the Christ, the Eternal God." (2 Nephi 26:12.) This message was selected by Moroni to be included on the title page of the Book of Mormon. Since the Gentiles are those who already believe in Jesus Christ, the significance must be his designation as "the Eternal God." Although they already accept him to one degree or another, they do not accept him as taught in the Book of Mormon, as the creator and administrator of the earth and its people. By way of warning, Moroni told the Gentiles to "serve the God of the land, who is Jesus Christ" or they would be swept off. (Ether 2:10-12.)

Nephi further attested that Jesus "manifesteth himself unto all those who believe in him, by the power of the Holy Ghost; yea, unto every nation, kindred, tongue, and people, working mighty miracles, signs, and wonders." (2 Nephi 26:13.)

Nephi also prophesied that in the day when the Book of Mormon would come forth, the churches that were not built up to the Lord would contend with each other, teach their own doctrines, and deny the Holy Ghost. He said further that these churches would claim that the Lord had done his work and given his power unto men. Nephi also foretold their denying miracles in this day. (2 Nephi 28:4-6). All these characteristics are observable in various churches today. Therefore, the Book of Mormon is an ensign, a witness, to the Gentiles that they must seek after the Holy Ghost to escape the impending doom. Further, if they will seek him, they will experience miracles, signs, and wonders in their lives.

Moroni admonished the Gentiles not to mock the Book of Mormon. He promised them that faith, hope, and charity would bring them to Christ, "the fountain of all righteousness." (Ether 12:22-28.) Moroni also prayed for grace for the Gentiles, that they might have charity. Then he commended them to "seek this Jesus of whom the prophets and apostles have written, that the grace of God the Father, and also the Lord Jesus Christ, and the Holy Ghost, which beareth record of them, may be and abide in you forever." (Ether 12:36-41.)

Moroni gave two more admonitions to the Gentiles. He warned them to not allow secret combinations to get power over them, (Ether 8:23-26) and he recorded the promise of the Lord that if they would accept the Book of Mormon and come to Him, He would show them "greater things, the knowledge which is hid up because of unbelief." (Ether 4:6-13.) This is probably a reference to the sealed portion of the plates that was not translated. (See D&C 5:4-10; Ether 4:7.)

Thus, many blessings are promised to the Gentiles. But, as foretold by the Lord, many of them will not receive these blessings, or, as Joseph Smith said, few will accept them.[4] We should pray as did Moroni that they will accept. We should also use our efforts to raise the Book of Mormon as an ensign and give them the opportunity to be numbered with the house of Israel as they were invited to do by Mormon. (3 Nephi 30:1-2.)

6

An Ensign to the Lamanites

The Lord promised Enos that the gospel would be restored in His own due time through the Nephite records. Those records, the Book of Mormon, have come forth as an ensign to the Lamanites. The Lord informed Enos that he wasn't the only one who had received this promise, because his fathers had also prayed for it. (Enos 1:12-18.) Since Enos was the son of Jacob who was the son of Lehi, the "fathers" mentioned by the Lord would be Jacob and Lehi. Nephi, brother of Jacob, also knew of this restoration from the brass plates, and he noted that many of the prophets of old had known of the Lamanites. Nephi included some of their prophecies with his own records, as did subsequent Nephite prophets. From the combined knowledge of the Old Testament and the Nephite prophets revealed in the Book of Mormon, the present-day reader can see the destiny of this remnant of the house of Israel.

Nephi knew that the Lord had shown many of the ancient prophets concerning his people. (1 Nephi 19:21.) While the context seems to refer to Nephi's people being led to their new land, it is the words of Isaiah that foretell the destiny of his people in the Americas and their eventual return to the knowledge that the Lord is their Savior and Redeemer, "the Mighty One of Jacob." (1 Nephi 21; Isaiah 49; note particularly verses 1 Nephi 21: 22-26 and Nephi's explanation in 1 Nephi 22:6-12.)

One of the many Old Testament prophets who knew the destiny of the Nephites and Lamanites was Joseph of Egypt. This

Joseph, the patriarch of the Nephites and Lamanites, prophesied that his seed would be brought "out of darkness unto light—yea, out of hidden darkness and out of captivity unto freedom." (2 Nephi 3:5.) Joseph's father, Jacob, the father of the twelve tribes of Israel, was also aware that the seed of Joseph would be in the Americas. He blessed Joseph that some of his branches (descendants) would run over the wall (of the ocean) "unto the utmost bound of the everlasting hills." (Genesis 49:22-26.)

This interpretation is supported by the Lord's description of the Nephite people to Jacob, brother of Nephi, as "a righteous branch from the fruit of the loins of Joseph" that he had led out of the land of Jerusalem. (Jacob 2:25.) Furthermore, the Savior commented to the Nephites that the covenant he had made with their father, Jacob, would be fulfilled by the establishment of the Nephite people in America. (3 Nephi 20:22.)

Another Old Testament prophet who was fully aware of the Nephites and Lamanites was Zenos. His great prophecies are no longer in the Bible, but at least some of them have been restored through the Book of Mormon. (See 1 Nephi 19:10-16; Jacob 5.) Samuel the Lamanite verified that "the prophet Zenos, and many other prophets" spoke "concerning the restoration of our brethren the Lamanites, again to the knowledge of the truth" after they were driven, smitten, and scattered abroad. The Lamanites, according to Zenos, "shall again be brought to the true knowledge, which is the knowledge of their Redeemer, and their great and true shepherd, and be numbered among his sheep." (Helaman 15:11-13.) This true knowledge will come through the Book of Mormon, the ensign the Lord has prepared for them.

In addition to these Old Testament prophets to whom Nephi referred, most of the Book of Mormon seers recorded prophecies of the latter-day restoration among the Lamanites. The Savior also spoke extensively to the Nephites of this restoration when he visited the Americas.[1]

Who Are the Lamanites?

The term *Lamanite* refers to many different groups in the Book of Mormon. These need to be identified to help us understand to whom the Book of Mormon ensign is to be raised.

After the death of Lehi (2 Nephi 4:12), the Lord warned Nephi that he and his family should depart from his elder brethren, who were angry with him, "and flee into the wilderness." (2 Nephi 5:1-5.) The families of Zoram, Laban's servant; Sam, Nephi's brother; Nephi's younger brothers Jacob and Joseph; his sisters; "and all those who would go" went with Nephi into the wilderness and called themselves "the people of Nephi." (2 Nephi 5:6-9.) Whether or not some of Laman's and Lemuel's children or any of Ishmael's family went with Nephi is not stated. Nephi called the entire group Nephites, or "those who believed in the warnings and the revelations of God." (2 Nephi 5:6.)

The Lamanites, those who remained behind to follow Laman, were later characterized by Jacob, brother of Nephi, as those "that seek to destroy the people of Nephi." Jacob characterized the Nephites as "the people who were not Lamanites" or "those who are friendly to Nephi." (Jacob 1:13-14.) Note that the families or tribes of each brother, the servant Zoram, and the Ishmaelites had been kept separate. The listing of these families implies that the family of Ishmael had remained with Laman and Lemuel, because they are listed by Jacob following the Lamanites and Lemuelites. Later, according to Alma 43:13, the sons of Ishmael were part of the Lamanites.

However, the two groups were not strictly divided by family or tribe. From the time of the separation into Nephites and Lamanites, there were many who left one group and became part of the other. Such groups as the Amlicites, the Amalekites, the Zoramites, and the descendants of King Noah dissented from the Nephites and became Lamanites. These were nearly as numerous as the Nephites. (Alma 43:13-14.) Those who "suffered [themselves] to be led away by the Lamanites [were] called under that head, and there was a mark set upon [them]." (Alma 3:10.) Those Lamanites who were converted and joined with the Nephites "were no more called Lamanites" but were numbered among the Nephites and distinguished by such names as "Anti-Nephi-Lehies" or "the people of Ammon." (Alma 23:17; 27:26-27.)

After the Savior's visit to the Americas, the term *Lamanite* had another designation. All but the more righteous were destroyed at Christ's coming (3 Nephi 10:12), and all those remaining were "converted unto the Lord, upon all the face of the land, both Nephites and Lamanites." (4 Nephi 1:2.) Consequently, "neither were there Lamanites, nor any manner of -ites; but they were in one, the children of Christ, and heirs to the kingdom of God." (4 Nephi 1:17.) This conversion took place from A.D. 34 to 36, but by A.D. 111, there were "a small part of the people who had revolted from the church and taken upon them the name of Lamanites; therefore there began to be Lamanites again in the land." (4 Nephi 1:20.)

By A.D. 231, this revolt had grown until "there was a great division among the people." Those who "were true believers in Christ" were called Nephites, and those "who rejected the gospel were called Lamanites, and Lemuelites, and Ishmaelites." (4 Nephi 1:35-39.) While it is often stated that this division was primarily one of ideology and not of bloodline, a close examination of the scriptures shows that the bloodline was still a prevalent factor in this division. The Nephites were called "Jacobites, and Josephites, and Zoramites" by the Lamanites. The Lamanites were those who willfully rebelled against the gospel of Christ, and they taught "their children that they should not believe, [and] even as their fathers from the beginning, did dwindle." (4 Nephi 38.) The phrase "even as their fathers" strongly suggests family connections.

Although the post-Zion separation was apparently primarily along bloodlines, there was still much desertion of the Nephites to the Lamanites. (Moroni 9:24.) Desertions continued to increase until the final destruction of the Nephites in the fourth generation after the visit of Christ. Those Nephites who were not destroyed were "numbered among the Lamanites" and became "like unto them, all, save it be a few who [were] called the disciples of the Lord"; these the Lamanites pursued until they became extinct, as had been prophesied by Alma. (Alma 45:12-14.) Moroni was the last Nephite to survive that Lamanite pursuit. (Moroni 1:1-2.)

The Nephite dissension and desertion was extensive enough that descendants of all of Lehi's sons as well as of Zoram and of Ishmael were part of the Lamanites. That descendants of all the original families of Lehi's group are among the Lamanites today has been confirmed by modern-day revelation. (D&C 3:16-18.) This preservation was part of the fulfillment of the Lord's promises to Enos and other Nephites that the Lamanites might also know of the promises extended to them for their salvation. (D&C 3:19-20.) The fulfillment of the rest of the promises, that a record would be preserved and brought forth to the Lamanites (speaking collectively of all those who remained) in the latter days (Enos 1:11-18) is fulfilled by the Book of Mormon, an ensign to the Lamanites. Latter-day revelation verifies that the Book of Mormon fulfills the promise made to the Nephite fathers. (D&C 10:46-52.)

The Fall of the Nephite Nation

The fall of the Nephites is a warning to today's Lamanites, many of whom are descendants of those fallen Nephites, of the obstacles they must avoid or overcome.

Nephi, son of Lehi, gave two reasons why the Nephites would fall. He saw in vision that the seed of his brethren, the Lamanites (another indication that the post-Nephite Zion society Lamanites were primarily literal descendants of Laman and Lemuel), were able to overpower his seed because of pride and the temptations of the devil. (1 Nephi 12:19). He saw that those who were not overpowered, both Lamanites and Nephites, would dwindle in unbelief and become an idle people full of abominations. (1 Nephi 12:23.) Nephi later commented on this vision, giving the same two reasons for the "speedy destruction" as the "reward of their pride and their foolishness" and their yielding "unto the devil" and having chosen "works of darkness rather than light." (2 Nephi 26:10.) Because of these situations, Nephi said, "The Spirit of the Lord will not always strive with man. And when the Spirit ceaseth to strive with man then cometh speedy destruction." (2 Nephi 26:11.)

Mormon, after personally witnessing the fall that Nephi had seen in vision, gave the same two reasons for the Nephite demise, although in slightly different words. Mormon listed the Lamanites' "unbelief and idolatry," another way of defining pride, as one of the reasons. He next listed "the Spirit of the Lord" having "ceased to strive with their fathers," and their being "led about by

Satan" rather than by Christ and God as they had previously been led. (Mormon 5:16-18.) Therefore, the Lamanites today must humble themselves, believe in Christ, and avoid worshipping idols in their cultures or inherited from the culture of the Gentiles. Furthermore, they must avoid secret conspiracies and engage in worthwhile pursuits rather than being idle. This will help them to have the Spirit of the Lord guide their everyday actions. Following this course will bring them the blessings of Joseph, to which they are rightful heirs.

The Promises of the Restoration

Alma the younger said: "There are many promises which are extended to the Lamanites; for it is because of the traditions of their fathers that caused them to remain in their state of ignorance; therefore the Lord will be merciful unto them and prolong their existence in the land." (Alma 9:16; see also Helaman 15:10-13.) One of these promises extends back over 3,500 years.

The Lord covenanted with Joseph that he "would raise up a righteous branch unto the house of Israel; not the Messiah, but a branch which was to be broken off." Lehi recognized the fulfillment of this covenant through his people, but he also noted that Joseph had been promised that the Messiah would not be manifested to this branch until the latter days. Two things were to be accomplished through this manifestation: they were to be brought "out of darkness unto light," and they were to be brought "out of captivity unto freedom." (2 Nephi 3:5.) The first deliverance is spiritual; the second, political.

The spiritual dimension will come about through the restoration of the Book of Mormon as an ensign to the Lamanites. Nephi summarized his commentary on the future of his seed and the seed of his brethren (2 Nephi 25:23-26:11) by stating that after the Book of Mormon would come forth, the remnant of their seed would know concerning them, how they came out from Jerusalem, and that they were descendants of the Jews. (2 Nephi 30:3-4.)[2] Nephi said: "The gospel of Jesus Christ shall be declared among them; wherefore, they shall be restored unto the knowledge of their fathers, and also to the knowledge of Jesus Christ, which was had among their fathers." (2 Nephi 30:5.) That this would not be an immediate restoration was also known by Nephi. He said that this blessing "from the hand of God" would cause the "scales of darkness" to "begin to fall from their eyes; and many generations [should] not pass away among them, save they [should] be a pure[3] and a delightsome people." (2 Nephi 30:6.) The scales' "beginning" to fall from their eyes implies that this would be just the beginning and not the end. The "not many generations" implies that it would not be a long time until it was completed. The "pure and delightsome people" suggests they would become a zion people as foretold in their ensign, the Book of Mormon. (3 Nephi 20:22.)

Some believe that the Lamanites will build the New Jerusalem upon the American continent. However, the Book of Mormon teaches otherwise. When the Savior visited the Nephites, he quoted the Father as saying that "the remnant of Jacob, unto whom I have given this land for their inheritance" would build the New Jerusalem. (3 Nephi 21:22-23.) America was given to the remnant of the house of Joseph. (3 Nephi 15:12-13.) This is usually assumed to be the Lamanites. However, on June 7, 1831, the members of The Church of Jesus Christ of Latter-day Saints were called by the Lord "a remnant of Jacob, and those who are heirs according to the covenant." (D&C 52:2.) The remnants of Jacob are also the remnants of Joseph, and most church members are of the lineage of Joseph through either Ephraim or Manasseh. Being the birthright holder would qualify Ephraim as the heir according to the covenant.

On his visit to the Nephites, the Savior further quoted the Father about the gospel's not being preached among the majority of the Lamanites until after the building of the New Jerusalem. (3 Nephi 21:26.) While many of the Lamanites are having the ensign lifted to them today, millions of them in South and Central America have not yet had that opportunity. The New Jerusalem will be built by the remnant of Jacob who are members of The Church of Jesus Christ of Latter-day Saints and "also as many of the house of Israel as shall come." (3 Nephi 21:23.) These could include some of the Lamanites who have been converted, but the direction of the building would be under those who hold the keys of this dispensation—the leadership of The Church of Jesus

Christ of Latter-day Saints.[4] As the Lamanites are converted and
brought into the New Jerusalem, Zion, and her stakes, they will
become pure in heart and be delivered out of darkness unto light
in fulfillment of prophecy.

There is a further fulfillment of the spiritual deliverance of the
Lamanites as quoted by Nephi from Isaiah: the Gentiles will become nursing fathers and mothers to the Lamanites. (Isaiah
49:22-23; 1 Nephi 21:22-23.) Part of this nourishment will be the
bringing forth of the Book of Mormon, their ensign, and the restoration of the gospel among the Gentiles who will take it to the
Lamanites. (1 Nephi 22:6-9; 3 Nephi 21:5-10.) However, when
those Gentiles reject this marvelous work that has come forth
among them, then will come the time for the Lamanites to be delivered "out of captivity unto freedom." (2 Nephi 3:5.)

The rejection of the ensign by the Gentiles will bring about
the fulfillment of Moses' prophecy that whoever would not hearken to the Lord's word (including the Book of Mormon) would be
cut off from among the Lord's covenant people. (3 Nephi 21:11;
Deuteronomy 18:19; Acts 3:23.) Those who are thus cut off
(many of the Gentiles will accept the work and be numbered with
Israel) will be trodden down by the Lamanites as the Savior
foretold. The Lamanites will thus be delivered from the bondage
of the Gentiles. The Savior quoted the words of Micah to illustrate this trodding down to the Nephites. (3 Nephi 21:12-21;
Micah 5:8-15.)[5] This is also confirmed in modern-day revelation
(D&C 87:5-6) and by a latter-day prophet.[6] It should be noted
that this same prophecy will be fulfilled with other tribes of the
house of Israel (see 2 Nephi 6:8-18), but the fulfillment of this
prophecy will complete the first promise to the Lamanites that
they will become a righteous branch of the house of Israel.

A second promise to the Lamanites was that in the latter days
the fulness of the gospel would come to them from the Gentiles.
(1 Nephi 15:13.) This was also given by the Savior as a sign to the
Nephites of the gathering of Israel in the latter days. (3 Nephi
21:1-7.) The Gentiles who were to bring the gospel are, of course,
cultural Gentiles, those who are living among the Gentiles even
though they are of the house of Israel.[7] The gospel they were to

bring would be in the Book of Mormon that the Lamanites would look to as an ensign.

Nephi lists four things the Lamanites are to come to know through the restoration of the fulness of the gospel. (See 1 Nephi 15:14-15.) The first thing that the Lamanites are to know is that they are of the house of Israel and are thus the covenant people of the Lord. This point was also the first thing Mormon noted as he wrote his final words on the plates. (Mormon 7:1-2, 10.)

Second, Nephi said they were to come to "the knowledge of their forefathers." (1 Nephi 15:14.) This knowledge was to include an awareness that they came from Jerusalem. (2 Nephi 30:4; 33:8.) From Mormon's admonitions, we learn that the major reason they need this knowledge about Jerusalem is to bring them to a knowledge of Jesus Christ and his mission among the Jews. (Mormon 7:5.)

Third, Nephi said they were to come to "the knowledge of the gospel of their Redeemer which was ministered unto their fathers by him . . . and the very points of his doctrine." (1 Nephi 15:14; 2 Nephi 30:5.) In other words, they were to come to understand the gospel as taught in the Book of Mormon, their ensign. (See also Helaman 15:13-16.) Mormon later enumerated these points of doctrine for them: having faith in the resurrection of Christ and in the redemption of the world through Jesus Christ; repenting and being baptized as taught in both the Bible and the Book of Mormon; and believing in both of these records. (Mormon 7:3, 5-9.)

The final point of Nephi's prophecy was that the Lamanites would come to rejoice and receive "strength and nourishment from the true vine." The source of this nourishment would be "the true fold of God," or the Church. (1 Nephi 15:15.) The true vine is identified in the Gospel of John as Jesus Christ. (John 15:5.) The fulfillment of these four blessings would cause them to be remembered again among the house of Israel. (1 Nephi 15:16.)

The Promises Fulfilled

Just when these promises to the Lamanites would be fulfilled, both generally and specifically, is made very clear in the Book of

Mormon. Nephi said the restoration was not to come "until after they [were] scattered by the Gentiles." This was so "the Lord may show his power unto the Gentiles" (1 Nephi 15:17) or, as Lehi said, after the Gentiles had received the fulness of the gospel (1 Nephi 10:14).

The specific time of the fulfillment of the promises to the Lamanites is after the building of the New Jerusalem in America. (3 Nephi 21:23.) This specific time was given by the Savior himself. Although many Lamanites will have accepted the gospel before this event, the majority of them will not receive the gospel until after it. From the Doctrine and Covenants we know that the New Jerusalem will be built in Independence, Missouri. (D&C 57:3.) Therefore, when the New Jerusalem is built, the work among the Lamanites will greatly accelerate.

Just as important as when these promises will be fulfilled is how they will be fulfilled. Of course, the primary source of this information is the Book of Mormon, the ensign to the Lamanites. After bearing witness of Jesus Christ as the only name under heaven whereby salvation would come, Nephi said: "For this cause hath the Lord God promised unto me that these things which I write shall be kept and preserved, and handed down unto my seed, from generation to generation, that the promise may be fulfilled unto Joseph, that his seed should never perish as long as the earth should stand." (2 Nephi 25:20-21.) Nephi further prophesied that his writings would go to other nations "according to the will and pleasure of God," but all their diligent labor of writing was meant to persuade their children, and also their brethren, to believe in Christ. (2 Nephi 25:22-23.) The Lord promised these things not only to Nephi but also to Enos and others. (Enos 1:16-18.) Mormon bore similar testimony that the Book of Mormon would be the primary source of the conversion of "the seed of this people." (Mormon 5:15.)

Another source for teaching the gospel to the Lamanites is the Bible, or the record of the Jews. Nephi saw in vision that the Bible would come to the remnant of his seed from the Gentiles before other records (the Book of Mormon, Doctrine and Covenants, and Pearl of Great Price) would come to "establish the truth of the first." (1 Nephi 13:38-41.) Nephi further testified that "the Jews shall have the words of the Nephites, and the Nephites shall have the words of the Jews." (2 Nephi 29:13.)

The Book of Mormon also bears witness of two people who will be instruments in the hand of the Lord in restoring the Lamanites to their promised blessings. The first person is the Prophet Joseph Smith, called in the Book of Mormon "a choice seer." The Lord promised Joseph of Egypt, "A choice seer will I raise up out of the fruit of thy loins." (2 Nephi 3:7.) Joseph Smith was to direct the work of taking the gospel to the Lamanites. Of course, many others would assist, which would fulfill the Savior's, Lehi's, and Nephi's declarations that the gospel would come forth from the cultural Gentiles. (3 Nephi 21:5; 1 Nephi 15:17.)

The other person who the Book of Mormon testifies will do a great work among the Lamanites is a descendant of Joseph, son of Lehi. Many people interpret this to be Joseph Smith, but a careful reading shows another possible interpretation. The prophecy of this person was made by Lehi as he gave his final blessing and admonition to his son Joseph. Joseph was promised that his "seed [should] not utterly be destroyed." (2 Nephi 3:3.) Lehi substantiated this promise through the covenants made to Joseph of Egypt and then prophesied to his son: "Thy seed shall not be destroyed, for they shall hearken unto the words of the book [the Book of Mormon]. And there shall rise up one mighty among them [the seed of Joseph, son of Lehi], who shall do much good, both in word and in deed, being an instrument in the hands of God, with exceeding faith, to work mighty wonders, and do that thing which is great in the sight of God, unto the bringing to pass much restoration unto the house of Israel, and unto the seed of thy brethren." (2 Nephi 3:23-24.) This obviously is not Joseph Smith but a Lamanite leader.[8] What this work will include or when it will be accomplished is not specified, but it is logical to expect it to come when the majority of the Lamanites are restored to their promised blessings, which will be after the building of the New Jerusalem.

The Messages to the Lamanites

There are three basic messages to the Lamanites in their ensign, the Book of Mormon. The first was recorded by Nephi as an admonition to his people. He said: "The right way is to believe in Christ, and deny him not; and Christ is the Holy One of Israel; wherefore ye must bow down before him, and worship him with all your might, mind, and strength, and your whole soul; and if ye do this ye shall in nowise be cast out." (2 Nephi 25:29.) Before this admonition, Nephi bore witness of the relationship that the people of his day had with Christ, and after the admonition, he foretold the future destiny of the Nephites. (2 Nephi 25:24–26:11.) While much is said about Christ throughout the Book of Mormon, Nephi's statement is a good summary of its message about Christ.

The second basic message to the Lamanites is to believe both the Book of Mormon and the Bible. Nephi told his beloved brethren, the Jews, and all the ends of the earth: "Hearken unto these words and believe in Christ; and if ye believe not in these words believe in Christ. And if ye shall believe in Christ ye will believe in these words, for they are the words of Christ, and he hath given them unto me; and they teach all men that they should do good." (2 Nephi 33:10.) Nephi further testified that those who came to a knowledge of the Book of Mormon would know at the judgment bar that he had been commanded to write those words. (2 Nephi 33:11-15.)

As Moroni concluded his writings to the Lamanites, he admonished: "When ye shall read these things, if it be wisdom in God that ye should read them, [I would] that ye would remember how merciful the Lord hath been unto the children of men, from the creation of Adam even down until the time that ye shall receive these things, and ponder it in your hearts." (Moroni 10:3.) The only way they could know of God's mercy from Adam down to the time they would receive the Book of Mormon would be through studying the Bible. As they study the Bible, they will find it to be a companion volume to the Book of Mormon. Thus Moroni's testimony is added to Nephi's and Mormon's above.

The third basic message to the Lamanites is given by Moroni. The book called by his name and placed at the end of the plates was written that it "may be of some worth unto my brethren, the Lamanites, in some future day, according to the will of the Lord." (Moroni 1:4.) Moroni admonishes his people to "ask God, the

Eternal Father, in the name of Christ if these things are not true."
He then gives them some qualifications for knowing through the
power of the Holy Ghost of the truth of the Book of Mormon and
of the Bible. (Moroni 10:4-5.) Following these qualifications, he
discusses the various gifts of the Spirit through which the power of
God may manifest to them that the Book of Mormon and Bible
are true. (Moroni 10:7-26.) He then adds testimony similar to
Nephi's that he, Moroni, will be at the bar of God and that God
will say, "Did I not declare my words unto you, which were written by this man, like as one crying from the dead, yea, even as one
speaking out of the dust?" (Moroni 10:27-34.) Those who follow
Moroni's admonition will rejoice as they meet Moroni at the judgment bar.

7

An Ensign to the Jews

The Lord, in the Book of Mormon and other scriptures, has revealed that the gospel is to be preached to the Jews in the latter days. Much is shown concerning how this is to be done and even to some extent where it will commence, but the specific time the full program will be inaugurated among the Jews has yet to be revealed.

On August 6, 1833, the Lord revealed to Joseph Smith that the Saints were to "renounce war and proclaim peace" and to "turn the hearts of the Jews unto the prophets, and the prophets unto the Jews." (D&C 98:16-17.) This commandment can be fulfilled through the Book of Mormon, an ensign to the Jews.

Many Old Testament prophecies concern the Book of Mormon.[1] Through relating these prophecies to the Jewish people among us and testifying of the coming forth of the Book of Mormon in fulfillment of these prophecies, we can help turn their hearts to the prophets who made these prophecies. Many will thus have a desire to read the marvelous work foretold by those prophets.

All the major contributors to the plates from which the Book of Mormon was translated spoke about the Jews or to the Jews.[2] Furthermore, Nephi considered his people to be Jews since they came out of Jerusalem. (2 Nephi 30:4; 33:8.)[3] He declared that he likened "all scripture unto us, that it might be for our profit and learning." (1 Nephi 19:23.) The likening of scripture to ourselves is figurative. Thus the hearts of the Book of Mormon prophets were turned to the Jews both literally and figuratively. As the members of the tribe of Judah are introduced to the Book of Mormon and read that sacred record, their hearts will also be turned to these Nephite prophets, and they will feel the peace of the Lord's Spirit in their hearts.

Furthermore, the Book of Mormon teaches about the law of war and principles governing those who are involved in war.[4] Although only a small part of the Jewish people live in the land of Palestine, where there is continual threat of or involvement in war, their unity brings the reality of war in that land to the hearts of those living elsewhere. The Book of Mormon teaches that peace comes through the combined efforts of the political leaders and the prophets. (See Words of Mormon 1:12-18; Ether 7:23-26.)

The Time Periods of Judah

The Book of Mormon speaks of three different time periods of the nation and people of Judah. These periods are the time of their destruction and captivity by Babylon, around 600 B.C.; the meridian of time; and the last days. The first two are now history. The third is now beginning.

The Babylonian Captivity

The Book of Mormon begins with a declaration that many prophets were warning of impending destruction by Babylon. (1 Nephi 1:4.) These prophets were Jeremiah, Zephaniah, Habakkuk, and possibly others, as evidenced from the Bible. Lehi, because of his positive response to those prophets, was shown in vision that Jerusalem would be destroyed, that many of its inhabitants would perish by the sword, and that many would be carried away captive into Babylon. (1 Nephi 1:13.) Lehi warned the people of Jerusalem of its impending destruction, but they rejected him, and the Lord instructed him to leave when they sought to kill him. (1 Nephi 1:18–2:2.)

After Lehi, Ishmael, and their families had left Jerusalem, they had faith in the prophecies of Jerusalem's destruction (1 Nephi 7:13-14); the fulfillment of the prophecies was later verified in vision to both Lehi and Jacob (2 Nephi 1:3-4; 6:8). This vision of Jerusalem's destruction was also verified when the Mulekites, who had come from Jerusalem at the time of its destruction, joined with the Nephites. (Omni 15-17; Helaman 8:21-22.)

The Jews who were taken captive into Babylon were allowed to return and build Jerusalem again, as had been prophesied by Jeremiah. (Jeremiah 25:8-14.) Lehi and Nephi had also prophesied that the Jews would return from Babylon in "the own due time of the Lord" and be restored "to the land of their inheritance." (1 Nephi 10:3; 2 Nephi 25:9-11.)

Thus, the Book of Mormon, as an ensign to the Jews, serves as a second witness of the Lord's hand in their destiny during Lehi's time. Further, it establishes the principle that the Lord warns people before their destruction but allows them their agency. Also, it shows that the Lord honors the covenant he has made to the Jews as part of his covenant people.

The Meridian of Time

The second period concerning the Jews deals primarily with the birth and ministry of Jesus Christ. Lehi prophesied that the Lord would raise up among the Jews "a Messiah, or in other words, a Savior of the world." (1 Nephi 10:4.) He also spoke of the many prophets who had testified of the Messiah.

Lehi also foretold of a prophet who would prepare the way before the Savior of the world and would baptize him. (1 Nephi 10:7-10.) The Book of Mormon text gives more detail of John the Baptist's ministry than does the present text of Isaiah. Whether Lehi was drawing on Isaiah's prophecy recorded in the brass plates or whether he was moved by the Spirit to give those further details is not mentioned. Nonetheless, they were fulfilled in the detail foretold by Lehi. (See Matthew 3:11; John 1:26-28.) This same vision was shown to Nephi. (1 Nephi 11:27.)

Nephi also wrote of the virgin birth of the Son of God and of his ministry. The angel who conversed with Nephi in this vision called the Savior "the Lamb of God, yea, even the Son of the Eternal Father." (1 Nephi 11:18-21.) Nephi was further shown the Lord's ministry of power and miracles. (1 Nephi 11:24-31.) He also saw that "the Son of the everlasting God was judged of the world" and "was lifted up upon the cross and slain for the sins of the world." (1 Nephi 11:32-33; see also 1 Nephi 19:7-12.)

Jacob, the brother of Nephi, was also shown these events (2 Nephi 6:9) and was told by an angel that the Redeemer's name would be Christ. He was further told that Christ would come into the more wicked part of the world because there was "none other nation on earth that would crucify their God." This the angel attributed to priestcrafts and iniquities. (2 Nephi 10:3-5.) That they practiced priestcraft certainly implies that the leadership of the Jewish nation was responsible for the Savior's death—not the people in general. This idea is supported by the New Testament. (See John 7:45-52; 8:33-59; 9:39-41; Matthew 23:13-36, noting the JST of verses 15, 24, 36, and JST Acts 3:18.)

Nephi was further shown that the house of Israel would fight against the twelve apostles of the Lamb. (1 Nephi 11:34-35.) This would certainly include the tribe of Judah and the other members of the house of Israel living in the southern kingdom, since the northern kingdom would long since have been taken away. The twelve apostles against whom Judah fought would be those called by Jesus in Palestine. The Jews' rejection of Christ and his apostles is attributed by Jacob to their having "despised the words of plainness, and killed the prophets, and sought for things that they could not understand." He said these problems were a blindness that "came by [their] looking beyond the mark." God then took "away his plainness from them, and delivered unto them many things which they [could not] understand, because they desired it." (Jacob 4:14.) Joseph Smith made this enlightening comment: "Many men will say, 'I will never forsake you, but will stand by you at all times.' But the moment you teach them some of the mysteries of the kingdom of God that are retained in the heavens and are to be revealed to the children of men when they are prepared for them they will be the first to stone you and put you to death. It was this same principle that crucified the Lord Jesus Christ, and will cause the people to kill the prophets in this generation."[5]

These descriptions by Jacob and Nephi seem to be an enlargement of the earlier declaration by the angel that priestcraft was one of the prime factors in the crucifixion.

Nephi's description of priestcraft as people preaching and setting "themselves up for a light unto the world, that they may get gain and praise of the world" (2 Nephi 26:29) is further evidence of the Jewish situation. The Jews were carried away in psuedo-intellectual pursuits and were ignoring the basic tenets of the gospel. (See D&C 19:31.) These pursuits accompanying their iniquities, also cited by Jacob (2 Nephi 10:5), led them to stumble and "reject the stone [Christ] upon which they might build and have safe foundation." (Jacob 4:15.)

Following this rejection of Christ, the Jews were scourged because they rejected "signs and wonders, and the power and glory of the God of Israel." (1 Nephi 19:13.) Following their scourging, those who remained were left to "wander in the flesh, and perish, and become a hiss and a by-word, and be hated among all nations," as was prophesied by Zenos. (1 Nephi 19:14; see also 2 Nephi 10:6.) This condition of the Jews was to be a sign to future generations that Jesus was indeed the Christ. This same condition was described by Isaiah as the Lord's refining the Jews "in the furnace of affliction." (Isaiah 48:10; 2 Nephi 20:10; see also 2 Nephi 6:10-11.) The symbolism of the refining process refers to the removal of impurities from their actions and thinking. The refinement was to occur while the Jews were scattered among the Gentiles. That these prophecies have been, are being, and will yet be fulfilled is obvious from a study of Jewish history. Their fulfillment is further attested to in modern revelation. (See D&C 133:35.)

The Last Days

The Book of Mormon also foretells of a final gathering, or restoration, of the Jews, after which "they should no more be confounded, neither should they be scattered again." (1 Nephi 15:20.) The gathering would occur in the day when they would believe in the Lord, that he was Christ. (2 Nephi 10:7.) Nephi said the gathering would start when they "shall begin to believe in Christ; and they shall begin to gather in upon the face of the land." (2 Nephi 30:7.) To "begin to believe in Christ" does not necessarily mean they will accept Jesus as their Messiah or as the Son of God. To begin to believe in Christ is to change their attitude toward him. This has certainly happened. Today, many branches of Judaism accept Jesus as a prophet or philosopher or teacher, although they do not look upon him as their Messiah. Many others (thousands) have forsaken their Jewish faith and joined Christian religions. However, the Christian religions of today do not have the fulness of the gospel Jesus said would be preached among the Jews.

"Beginning to gather" is in conjunction with "beginning to believe," and both are under way. While several million Jews have returned to their promised land in the last hundred years, they are only a small percentage of the many Jews scattered throughout the world. Those who have returned have been involved in restoring a political unit, but the full restoration of the Jews will not occur until the gospel is restored among them. This will fulfill Jacob's prophecy of their being "gathered in from their long dispersion, from the isles of the sea, and from the four parts of the earth." He also said: "The nations of the Gentiles shall be great in the eyes of me, saith God, in carrying them forth to the lands of their inheritance." (2 Nephi 20:8.) To further support this prophecy, Jacob quoted and commented on Isaiah's prophecy that the Gentiles would be nursing fathers and mothers to Judah as well as to the rest of the house of Israel. (Isaiah 49:22; 2 Nephi 10:9-22.)

The nursing of the house of Israel by the Gentiles has both a temporal and a spiritual fulfillment. (1 Nephi 22:6-9.) While the Jews have been under the political rule of Gentiles for years, and thus in this sense have been nursed by them, it is the spiritual nursing that will make the Gentiles great in the eyes of God. The Savior himself outlined this process when he visited the Nephites in America.

The gospel will be restored to the Jews after the Gentiles have received the fulness of the gospel but have hardened their hearts against the Lord. The Lord promised that he will then gather the Jews to their "promised land unto them forever." (3 Nephi 20:28-29.) This is a general or eventual promise.

The first step in the fulfillment of the promise is that the fulness of the gospel will be preached to the Jews. (3 Nephi 20:30.) This preaching will take place while they are still living among the Gentiles, as shown from the subsequent declaration that "then will the Father gather them together again, and give unto them Jerusalem for the land of their inheritance." (3 Nephi 20:33.) This preaching to the Jews among the Gentiles will thus be here in America and in other Gentile countries where the gospel has already been restored. This is consistent with President Spencer W. Kimball's admonition at a meeting of regional representatives on April 3, 1975, as reported in the *Ensign:*

> President Kimball next turned to another area of concern to him: the Jews. Noting that the gathering of the Jews to Jerusalem and the establishment of the gospel of Jesus Christ among them in this generation were set forth in great plainness in the scriptures, President Kimball said, "Is it not timely that we begin to preach to Judah as well as the other tribes?" Pointing out the fact that there are more Jews in the United States than in all the rest of the world, he continued: "Should we not now increase our effort to reach them? This does not mean a mission to Jerusalem in these troubled times, but we could begin to reach out for our Jewish brothers just as we do for all others."[6]

Those who have accepted the fulness of the gospel will believe that Jesus is the Son of God and pray to the Father in his name (3 Nephi 20:31; see also 2 Nephi 25:16), which is the next step outlined by the Savior.

The Savior then turned to the words of Isaiah for further details of the restoration of the Jews to their promised land. After the Jews accept Christ and his gospel, their own watchmen (priesthood holders or leaders) shall "lift up their voice, and with the voice together shall they sing; for they shall see eye to eye." (3 Nephi 20:32; Isaiah 52:8.) This suggests that the Jewish converts will join their voices with those who taught them and become the ones to teach others of their people. As they are converted, they will gather to Jerusalem, as they are instructed in the Doctrine and Covenants (133:13),[7] and build the city again as a holy city unto the Lord. (3 Nephi 20:34-40; Isaiah 52:9-10, 1-3, 7; Ether 13:5, 11; Moroni 10:31.)

However, as prophesied by Isaiah, this will not happen until the nation of Judah opens "the gates, that the righteous nation [restored Israel or the Church] which keepeth the truth may enter in." (Isaiah 26:2.) In other words, it will not be only by permission, but by request, that the gospel will be preached in Jerusalem. The Jewish converts from among the Gentiles will teach the gospel to the people who had previously gathered to Palestine. This may partially fulfill Isaiah's earlier prophecy that the word of the Lord will go out from Jerusalem. (Isaiah 2:3; 2 Nephi 12:3.) The Jews will then "be restored to the true church and fold of God; when they shall be gathered home to the lands of their inheritance, and shall be established in all their lands of promise," as foretold by Jacob. (2 Nephi 9:2.)[8] Jerusalem will then become a second world capital of the house of Israel as a complete fulfillment of Isaiah's prophecy.[9]

The Book of Mormon also cites Isaiah 51, in which Isaiah prophesied that because Judah would have no sons to guide her, two sons would come to testify to her and comfort her in her desolation and destruction. (2 Nephi 8:15-20; Isaiah 51:15-20.)[10] These are undoubtedly the two sons spoken of in Revelation 11. (See also D&C 77:14.) Elder LeGrand Richards said that these prophets would be called, ordained, and sent by the First Presidency of the Church.[11] Elder Bruce R. McConkie has identified them as members of the First Presidency or Quorum of the Twelve.[12] This prophecy will be fulfilled as the Gentiles are gathered against the Jews just before the appearance of Jesus Christ to the Jews, as spoken of by Zechariah (Zechariah 13:9-10; 14:1-9) and taught by the Savior to his disciples in the last week of his mortal life (See D&C 45:43-53; Matthew 24:1-4). Then all the Jews will know and recognize their long-awaited Messiah.

The Overall Messages

There are three basic messages in the Book of Mormon, an ensign, to the people of Judah.

The first message is really from Isaiah but is quoted by Nephi from the plates of brass. The Lord told Isaiah what would happen to the Jews so that they would not give credit for these events to false idols. (1 Nephi 20:3-8; Isaiah 48:3-8.)

The second message concerns a principle always followed by the Lord. Every generation of the Jews who have been destroyed had been warned by the Lord's prophets of their impending destruction. (2 Nephi 25:9.) Therefore the destruction was conditional upon their righteousness. They were therefore left without excuse.

The third message is the most important. It is that there is only one true Messiah and that the Jews "need not look forward any more for a Messiah to come." This Messiah is Jesus Christ, the only "name given under heaven . . . whereby man can be saved." (2 Nephi 25:18-20.) This Messiah had been prophesied by all the prophets since the beginning of the world. The Book of Mormon would persuade the Jews that Jesus is the Christ, the son of the living God. (Mormon 5:14; see also D&C 19:26-27.)

As Mormon concluded his abridgment of the Savior's ministry among the Nephites, he admonished readers to no "longer hiss, nor spurn, nor make game of the Jews, nor any of the remnant of the house of Israel." His admonition was based on his knowledge that the Lord would fulfill His covenant with Israel (3 Nephi 29:8.) The fulfillment of that covenant is under way. The Jews have been through their furnace of affliction. The Book of Mormon will bring them to the knowledge of their true Messiah. This knowledge will be verified at his second coming. Joseph Smith outlined what must take place before the Lord appears: "Judah must return, Jerusalem must be rebuilt, and the temple, and water come out from under the temple, and the waters of the Dead Sea be healed. It will take some time to rebuild the walls of the city and the temple, etc.; and all this must be done before the Son of Man will make His appearance."[13]

These things are well under way, but much more is yet to occur. The Jews have only begun to gather, and many more will yet gather. The rebuilding of Jerusalem has begun, but much is yet to be done.

8

An Ensign to the Lost Tribes

The allegory of the olive tree in Jacob specifies that three natural branches of Israel will be grafted back into the mother trunk
of the tame olive tree. (Jacob 5:39, 52-60.) The mother trunk is
the gathering of the birthright holders, Ephraim, and may be
identified as the Israelites who were scattered among the Gentiles.
The three groups which were to be grafted back will be in the reverse order of their having been taken away (Jacob 5:63), the lost
tribes, the tribe of Judah, and the Lamanites. The first group to
leave will be the last group grafted back. It is only logical that
some of the lost tribes remained together as a group. The grafting
back of a branch would have to be as a unit or a group and not
those in a scattered condition.

The lost tribes of Israel are those people of the northern part
of the divided kingdom following the reign of Solomon. They
were carried captive into Assyria about 722 B.C. (See 2 Kings
17:1-23.) This captivity had been predicted by the prophets and
especially by Isaiah.

When Isaiah was called to the ministry, he was told to make
the heart of the people (the Ten Tribes) fat, their ears heavy, and
to shut their eyes. Figuratively, this could mean to make the truth
so plain that the people would be left without excuse. Isaiah was
further told to continue warning "until the cities be without in-
habitant, and the houses without man, and land be utterly des-

79

olate; and the Lord have removed men far away, for there shall be a great forsaking in the midst of the land." (2 Nephi 16:9-12; Isaiah 6:9-12.) This prophecy was fulfilled when the ten northern tribes were taken captive into Assyria. Isaiah further prophesied that within sixty-five years of the threatened Syrio-Ephraimite war (traditionally dated 734 B.C.), Ephraim (the northern ten tribes) would "be broken that it be not a people." (2 Nephi 17:8; Isaiah 7:8.) History will undoubtedly confirm that at the end of those sixty-five years those ten and a half tribes left their Assyrian captivity and journeyed into the northland, as described in the Apocrypha:

> As for your seeing him gather to himself another multitude that was peaceable, these are the ten tribes which were led away from their own land into captivity in the days of King Hoshea whom Shalmaneser the king of the Assyrians led captive; he took them across the river, and they were taken into another land. But they formed a more distant region, where mankind had never lived, that there at least they might keep their statutes which they had not kept in their own land. And they went in by the narrow passages of the Euphrates river. For at that time the Most High performed signs for them, and stopped the channels of the river until they had passed over. Through that region there was a long way to go, a journey of a year and a half; and that country is called Arzareth.
>
> Then they dwelt there until the last times; and now, when they are about to come again, the Most High will stop the channels of the river again, so that they may be able to pass over. Therefore you saw the multitude gathered together in peace. But those who are left of your people, who are found within my holy border, shall be saved. Therefore when he destroys the multitude of the nations that are gathered together, he will defend the people who remain. And then he will show them very many wonders. (2 Esdras 13:40-47.)

Either on this northern expedition, or on their previous journey to Assyria, or on both occasions, this prophecy of Amos was fulfilled: "Behold, the eyes of the Lord are upon the sinful kingdom, and I will destroy it from off the face of the earth; saving that I will not utterly destroy the house of Jacob, saith the Lord. For, lo, I will command, and I will sift the house of Israel among all nations, like as corn is sifted in a sieve, yet shall not the least grain fall upon the earth." (Amos 9:8-9.)

As Nephi prophesied, "the house of Israel, sooner or later, will be scattered upon all the face of the earth and also among all nations." (1 Nephi 22:3.)

Those who were scattered among all nations are basically the Ephraimites who have already been gathered and others of Ephraim and the other tribes who will yet be gathered from the Gentile nations.

A Branch of Israel

The Book of Mormon teaches that a group of the ten tribes remained intact. When the Savior visited the Nephites, he identified the Nephites as some of those who had been separated from their brethren in Jerusalem because of the iniquity of the Jews, and he further said that "other tribes hath the Father separated from them [the Jews]; and it is because of their iniquity that they know not of them." (3 Nephi 15:19-20.) The Savior also identified the Nephites as part of the other sheep whom he had told the people in Jerusalem that he would visit. (John 10:14-16; 3 Nephi 15:21-24.) He then said that there were other tribes neither of Jerusalem nor of the Nephites that he was commanded of the Father to visit, these being the lost tribes. Though they are lost to us, Jesus said they were not lost to the Father. (3 Nephi 17:4.)

The Nephites were commanded to write these sayings as a witness to the Gentiles "that through the fulness of the Gentiles, the remnant of their seed, who shall be scattered forth upon the face of the earth because of their [Jews'] unbelief, may be brought in, or may be brought to a knowledge of me, their Redeemer." (3 Nephi 16:4.) Following this gathering of the Jews from among the Gentiles, the Savior will gather the ten tribes from the four quarters of the earth and fulfill the covenant the Father made to all the people of the house of Israel. (3 Nephi 16:1-5.) Jesus announced: "I go unto the Father, and also to show myself unto the lost tribes of Israel, for they are not lost unto the Father, for he knoweth whither he hath taken them." (3 Nephi 17:4.)

Obviously a group of the ten tribes was still gathered as a unit of some kind in the meridian of time. It also seems evident that some of these people would remain together and be gathered in the last days as part of the gathering of Israel in order to graft a branch back into the mother tree. This is consistent with other teachings in the Book of Mormon.

The Return of the Lost Tribes

The various theories of the location of this group will not be treated here. Where they are will be known only when, as Nephi said, Isaiah's prophecies "shall be fulfilled." (2 Nephi 25:7.) The Book of Mormon, however, does add more light to the events of their return. In the Book of Mormon, the Lord testified that he would speak to the Jews, to the Nephites, and to the other tribes of the house of Israel that he had led away, and all would write his words. He further testified: "The Jews shall have the words of the Nephites, and the Nephites shall have the words of the Jews; and the Nephites shall have the words of the lost tribes of Israel; and the lost tribes of Israel shall have the words of the Nephites and the Jews." (2 Nephi 29:11-13.) There is no record today of the Savior's visit to the lost tribes. So, when the lost tribes return, they will bring their record with them or it will be restored.

The Book of Mormon quotes a prophecy of Isaiah about the return of the ten tribes. Isaiah said there would "be a highway for the remnant of his people which shall be left, from Assyria." (2 Nephi 21:16; Isaiah 11:16.) This is further amplified in the Doctrine and Covenants (section 133; see also JST Isaiah 34:8-10). An interpretation of this section will not be given here. It is sufficient to say that the Book of Mormon contains a prophecy of the return of the lost tribes that is consistent with the idea that they will return, at least in part, as a group.[1]

Another indication that the ten tribes still exist as a group is from the Prophet Joseph Smith. In June 1831, he reportedly made this interesting prophecy, as reported by John Whitmer: "The spirit of the Lord fell upon Joseph in an unusual manner, and he prophesied that John the Revelator was then among the Ten Tribes of Israel who had been led away by Shalmaneser, king of Assyria, to prepare them for their return from their long dispersion, to again possess the land of their fathers. He prophesied many more things that I have not written."[2]

The Savior taught the Nephites that the work of the Father would commence among all the dispersed of his people, even the tribes that had been lost, after the building of the New Jerusalem in America. (3 Nephi 21:23-26.) This event was explained as a fulfillment of Isaiah's prophecy of the latter-day gathering. (3 Nephi 22:1-3; Isaiah 54:1-3.) On April 3, 1836, Moses appeared to Joseph Smith and Oliver Cowdery, committing to them the keys of the gathering of Israel from the four parts of the earth, and the leading of the ten tribes from the land of the north. (D&C 110:11.) Again, the gathering is separated into two parts—those gathered from the four parts of the earth or those dispersed among the nations, and the ten tribes returning from the land of the north. Their return seems to be the basis of the tenth article of faith written by the Prophet: "We believe in the literal gathering of Israel and in the restoration of the ten tribes."

The appearance of Moses further verifies that the keys of the lost tribes' return are held by the President of the Church today, and that their return will come about under his knowledge and direction. In the day it is fulfilled, the specifics of these prophecies will be known.

The Message to the Lost Tribes

When the ten tribes return, they will be given the record of the Nephites (the Book of Mormon) and the record of the Jews (the Bible). The Book of Mormon will be an ensign to them that we knew of their existence somewhere in the north countries, and that they were visited by the Savior in the meridian of time and have kept a record of that visit. Their record will serve as a third witness of Jesus Christ. The Book of Mormon will thus be an ensign to bring them into the Church and the New Jerusalem as other ensigns to the nations.

9

The New Jerusalem

The prophet Joseph Smith said: "We ought to have the building up of Zion as our greatest object."[1] The early revelations of this dispensation continually command us to "seek to bring forth and establish the cause of Zion." (D&C 6:6; 11:6; 12:6; 14:6.) The Book of Mormon teaches that Zion will be built, and it provides insights into how, when, and by whom this will be done. The term it usually uses for Zion is the *New Jerusalem.* Although many of the ideas in the Book of Mormon about the New Jerusalem are very general, its teachings are consistent with the revelations in the Doctrine and Covenants and the Pearl of Great Price. By correlating all these scriptures, we can obtain a more specific outline of how the New Jerusalem will be established.

What Is the New Jerusalem?

The New Jerusalem is a "holy sanctuary of the Lord" (Ether 13:3), a place where "the power of heaven" is in the midst of people who dwell therein; even Christ will be in their midst (3 Nephi 20:22). It is a place of gathering for the Lord's people, "an Holy City" where the inhabitants gird up their loins and look forward to the time of the Lord's Second Coming. (Moses 7:62.)

Many prophecies speak of the building of the New Jerusalem. Ether speaks of four such cities: the one built by Enoch, which was taken into heaven (Moses 7:18-21) but was to come back down

84

out of heaven (Ether 13:3); the one built by the Nephites after the coming of Christ (Ether 13:4; 4 Nephi); the Old Jerusalem, which would be "built up again, [and become] a holy city unto the Lord" (Ether 13:5, 11); and the one to be built in America to which the city of Enoch would return (Ether 13:6-9).

The Book of Mormon implies that the Jaredites had two such eras of righteousness. Under Emer, Coriantum, and Com were three righteous generations similar to the three generations of the Nephite Zion following Christ's ministry: both eras included judgment in righteousness, peace in the land, manifestations of Christ, physical progress, and living to an old age (Ether 9:14-25). Another period of four generations of righteousness was attained under Levi, Corom, Kish, and Lib. (Ether 10:16-29.) Thus, there are six possible Zion societies mentioned in the Book of Mormon text: Enoch's, that of the Nephites, the Old Jerusalem, the New Jerusalem in America, and the two possible Jaredite ones.

The people of Melchizedek also attained such a Zion society, according to the Joseph Smith translation of Genesis. (JST Genesis 14:32-34; see also Moses 7:27.) But our main concern will be the New Jerusalem that will be built in America before the Second Coming of Christ.

Where Will the New Jerusalem Be Built?

The Jaredite prophet Ether foretold the building of the latter-day New Jerusalem upon the Americas. He said further that it was to be built "unto the remnant of the seed of Joseph." (Ether 13:6-8.) This is consistent with the teachings of the Savior to the Nephites that the Father had given the land of America to them, a remnant of Joseph. (3 Nephi 15:12-13.) The same promise had been given hundreds of years earlier to Jacob, the father of the twelve tribes. The Savior also taught that the Father had established the Nephites in America to fulfill the covenant he had made with their father Jacob (the father of Joseph of Egypt—3 Nephi 20:20). Whether this covenant with Jacob refers to the blessing given by Jacob to his son Joseph concerning a branch going over the wall "unto the utmost bound of the everlasting hills" (Genesis 49:22-26) or to a different covenant with Jacob is not clear, but it seems logical that it is a separate covenant and the basis for Jacob's blessing upon his son.

The Book of Mormon does not specify where in the Americas the New Jerusalem will be built. However, the Lord revealed to Joseph Smith that "the place which is now called Independence [Missouri] is the center place" where Zion, or the New Jerusalem, will be built. (D&C 57:3; see also the introductory preface to section 57.)

Who Will Build the New Jerusalem?

Since the New Jerusalem is to be built "unto the remnant of Joseph," it is logical to think that the "remnant of Joseph" will build it. The Book of Mormon confirms this idea.

After abridging Ether's prophecy that a New Jerusalem would be built in America by a remnant of Joseph, Moroni spoke of there having been a type for this. He spoke of the Lord's bringing a remnant of Joseph's seed to the land of America, the land of their inheritance, where they would build up a holy city to the Lord. (Ether 13:6-8.)

The Savior, when he visited the Nephites, quoted the Father concerning the opportunities of the Gentiles. The Father said that the Gentiles who repented would have his church established among them, be brought into the covenant, and be numbered among the remnant of Jacob, to whom he had given the land for their inheritance. These converted Gentiles would then assist the Father's people (see 3 Nephi 20:46), "the remnant of Jacob, and also as many of the house of Israel as shall come, that they may build a city, which shall be called the New Jerusalem." (3 Nephi 21:22-23.)

A casual reading of this prophecy seems to suggest that the Lamanites will be the ones who will build this New Jerusalem. However, a careful study of other scriptures identifies the remnant of Jacob as any of the descendants of Joseph who have been preserved, not just those who are among the Lamanites in the last days. This would include most of the members of the Church today, who are primarily descendants of Ephraim. Furthermore, it is Ephraim who holds the birthright and thus has the responsibility to build the New Jerusalem.

Joseph Smith was described by Brigham Young as a pure Ephraimite, and this lineage was confirmed by President Joseph Fielding Smith.[2] Joseph Smith is undoubtedly the servant "unto whom rightly belongs the priesthood, and the keys of the kingdom," as identified in Doctrine and Covenants 113:6. These keys were given to the Church through him. (D&C 90:3-4.)

In June 1831, the Lord promised to consecrate the land of Missouri to his people, the members of the Church. He identified the Church members as his people "which are a *remnant of Jacob, and those who are heirs according to the covenant.*" (D&C 52:2, italics added.) Thus the Church, under the leadership of the prophet, seer, and revelator, who is a successor to Joseph Smith, and who will hold the keys at the time of the building of the New Jerusalem, will direct that work. The heirs, according to the covenant mentioned in Doctrine and Covenants 52:2, are the same as those included by the Savior as his Father's people and "as many of the house of Israel as shall come." (3 Nephi 21:23.)[3]

This does not mean that the Lamanites will not be involved. Certainly as descendants of Joseph they are also the inheritors of the land of America and will assist. But they will not be the only ones to build the city, and they will participate as members of the Church.

Not all members of the Church will build the New Jerusalem, however. As stated by the Lord in 1834, "There has been a day of calling, but the time has come for a day of choosing; and let those be chosen that are worthy. And it shall be manifest unto my servant, by the voice of the Spirit, those that are chosen." (D&C 105:35-36.) The day of calling was in 1831 when the Lord invited all to come to Missouri to build Zion, but the day of choosing is when the New Jerusalem shall be established by those who are given this charge. A select number of people will be chosen by the Lord through his Prophet to return to Jackson County and build the city. In the words of Brigham Young: "Remarks have been made as to our staying here. I will tell you how long we shall stay here. If we live our religion, we shall stay here in these mountains forever and forever, worlds without end, and a portion of the Priesthood will go and redeem and build up the center Stake of Zion."[4]

Those who are worthy and are chosen to go and redeem Zion may be identified further through the teachings of the Book of Mormon. The Nephite Zion society consisted of those who had "the love of God which did dwell in the hearts of the people. And there were no envyings, nor strifes, nor tumults, nor whoredoms, nor lyings, nor murders, nor any manner of lasciviousness . . . among all the people . . . but they were in one, the children of Christ and heirs to the kingdom of God." (4 Nephi 15-17.) Undoubtedly, these same qualifications will be required to be called to help build the New Jerusalem in Missouri.

A further description of the worthy was given by Isaiah and quoted by Jesus to the Nephites. They will be people who have "put on [their] strength" and have loosed themselves "from the bands of [their] neck, O captive daughter of Zion." (3 Nephi 20:36-37; Isaiah 52:1-2.) Those who put on the strength of Zion are "those whom God should call in the last days, who should hold the power of priesthood to bring again Zion, and the redemption of Israel; and to put on her strength is to put on the authority of the priesthood, which she, Zion, has a right to by lineage; also to return to that power which she had lost." (D&C 113:7-8.) The Lord further identified the loosing of the bands from the neck of Zion as the people who would overcome God's curses on "the remnants of Israel in their scattered condition among the Gentiles." In other words, they are those who have come out from spiritual Babylon, or the wickedness of the world, and follow the life of the Saints. (See D&C 133:14.) Therefore, worthy and dedicated Saints—members of the Church—will return to build the New Jerusalem.

How Will the New Jerusalem Be Built?

The New Jerusalem will be built by a Zion people. Those who established the New Jerusalem in Enoch's day were called Zion "because they were of one heart and one mind, and dwelt in righteousness; and there was no poor among them." (Moses 7:18.)

The same characteristics will bring about the latter-day Jerusalem, as is shown in the Book of Mormon.

In Nephi's vision of the nations and kingdoms of the Gentiles in the last days, the Lamb of God said: "Blessed are they who shall seek to bring forth my Zion at that day, for they shall have the gift and the power of the Holy Ghost." (1 Nephi 13:37.) The Holy Ghost will thus bring about the oneness of heart and mind required of a Zion people. The first characteristic a Zion people need is to be of one heart, to have the same goal, which, in this case, is the building of Zion. That this oneness is attained through the Holy Ghost is shown by the desires of the twelve disciples chosen by Jesus.

After Jesus visited the Nephites, the twelve disciples taught the multitude the things Jesus had taught them, and then they prayed "for that which they most desired," which was "that the Holy Ghost should be given unto them." (3 Nephi 19:9.) Following this prayer, they were baptized and were "filled with the Holy Ghost and with fire." (3 Nephi 19:13.) Jesus appeared among them and then prayed to the Father, thanking him for giving the Holy Ghost to those whom he had chosen. (3 Nephi 19:20.) Jesus continued his prayer: "Father, I pray not for the world, but for those whom thou has given me out of the world, because of their faith, that they may be purified in me, that I may be in them as thou, Father, art in me, that *we may be one,* that I may be glorified in them." (3 Nephi 19:29, italics added.) This prayer was answered, and they received a great outpouring of the Holy Ghost, which made them "white, even as Jesus." (3 Nephi 19:30.) Jesus prayed on in words that could not be spoken or written by man, yet the multitude "did understand in their hearts the words which he prayed." (3 Nephi 19:32-33.) This is the great example of the first characteristic of a Zion people—the Holy Ghost brings them a oneness of heart.

The Book of Mormon bears witness that to become of one mind is to become one in doctrine and beliefs. Nephi, son of Lehi, concluded his writing by teaching the doctrine of Christ. He bore record that the doctrine of Christ is "the only and true doctrine of the Father, and of the Son, and of the Holy Ghost, which is one

God without end." (2 Nephi 31:21.) This oneness is further exemplified through Jesus' visit to the Nephites. He commanded them that there should be no "disputations among [them] concerning the points of my doctrine, as there [had] hitherto been." (3 Nephi 11:28.) After declaring to them his doctrine, Jesus bore record that the doctrine came from the Father, and he said that those who believed in Christ would receive the Father's witness of Christ, for he would visit them with fire and the Holy Ghost. The Father, Son, and Holy Ghost would thus bear record of each other. Jesus then declared: "For the Father, and I, and the Holy Ghost are one." (3 Nephi 11:35-36.) Thus, through knowledge from the Holy Ghost, people can become one in the doctrine of Christ.

The third characteristic of Enoch's Zion people was that they dwelt in righteousness. To dwell in righteousness, as defined in the Book of Mormon, is to have the love of God "dwell in the hearts of the people." (4 Nephi 1:15.) When that happens, there are "no contentions and disputations among them, and every man . . . deal[s] justly one with another." They had peace and equality in the land, "not rich and poor, bond and free, but they were all made free, and partakers of the heavenly gift." (4 Nephi 1:2-3.) The heavenly gift referred to is, of course, the Holy Ghost, the source of the love of God dwelling in their hearts.

The Nephite Zion society had no poor among them, and neither did the society of Enoch before them. Poverty is overcome when the people live the law of God. President John Taylor said: "What does [Zion] mean? The pure in heart in the first place. In the second place those who are governed by the law of God—the pure in heart who are governed by the law of God."[5]

Although the Book of Mormon does not teach us about the law of God to be lived in Zion, the Doctrine and Covenants does. After the Saints were expelled from Jackson County, the Lord said that one reason for their expulsion was that they had not imparted "of their substance, as becometh saints, to the poor and afflicted among them; and [were] not united according to the union required by the law of the celestial kingdom; and Zion cannot be built up unless it is by the principles of the law of the celestial kingdom." (D&C 105:3-5.)

Continuing this revelation, the Lord revealed what must be accomplished before Zion is redeemed. He said that the lands in Jackson County, Missouri, and adjoining counties should be purchased, and that his Saints should possess them according to the laws of consecration he had given. (D&C 105:28-29.) These laws were to be "executed and fulfilled, after her [Zion's] redemption." (D&C 105:34.) Thus the law of God that eliminates poverty and qualifies one to live in Zion is the law of consecration.

When Will the New Jerusalem Be Built?

The Savior's teachings to the Nephites show that the New Jerusalem will be built after the people who will not believe in Christ will "be cut off from among [Christ's] people who are of the covenant." (3 Nephi 21:11; see also 20:23.) Jesus quoted the Father, further identifying those who would be cut off as those who would not repent and come to the Father's beloved Son. (3 Nephi 21:20).

Nephi, son of Lehi, saw this time in vision. He saw that among the Gentiles there would be two churches only, and he noted: "Whoso belongeth not to the church of the Lamb of God belongeth to that great church, which is the mother of abominations; and she is the whore of all the earth." (1 Nephi 14:10.) Nephi further beheld that the great mother of abominations gathered together "multitudes upon the face of all the earth, among all the nations of the Gentiles, to fight against the Lamb of God." However, the power of the Lamb of God "descended upon the saints of the church of the Lamb, and upon the covenant people of the Lord, who were scattered upon all the face of the earth; and they were armed with righteousness and with the power of God in great glory." (1 Nephi 14:13-14.) This description by Nephi is not limited only to the center place of Zion, Independence, Missouri (D&C 57:3), but it includes the whole earth. Those who do repent and come to Jesus will assemble in the stakes of Zion.

Further analysis shows that the stakes of Zion must be maintained to support the center place of Zion. The concept of stakes comes from the tent of Israel, which was transported and set up in the wilderness. According to the Savior's interpretation of Isaiah, this tent will be enlarged after the New Jerusalem is built (3 Nephi 22:2; Isaiah 54:2), but stakes must be established and maintained all the way around Jackson County before the center pole or place of the tent is raised. When this happens, the vision seen by Nephi will be fulfilled.

When the New Jerusalem is established and the great and abominable church is fighting against it, what will protect Zion? Isaiah, as quoted by Nephi, saw the day when the Lord would "create upon every dwelling place of Mount Zion, and upon her assemblies, a cloud and smoke by day and the shining of a flaming fire by night; for upon all the glory of Zion shall be a defence." This will be a place of refuge from the storm. (2 Nephi 14:5-6; Isaiah 4:5-6.) Note that this protection will be upon all the assemblies (or stakes), not just the center place.

A further indication of when the New Jerusalem would be built is given in the Book of Mormon. According to the Father's teachings that the Savior gave to the Nephites, the majority of the Lamanites and the tribes who had been lost (the ten tribes) would not be brought into the fold of God or the tent of Israel until after the New Jerusalem had been built. After that the work would commence among all nations. (3 Nephi 21:26-28.) This conversion of the Lamanites and the lost tribes will require the enlargement of Israel's tent, and it will fulfill the words of Isaiah as the Savior said. (3 Nephi 24:1-2.)

The prophets have described Zion as the whole of America, from north to south "where the mountain of the Lord [the temple] should be." They have also said "that it should be in the center of the land."[6] As the tent of Israel is enlarged, these prophecies will be fulfilled. But the work will not end there. In the words of Brigham Young, "Zion will extend, eventually, all over this earth. There will be no nook or corner upon the earth but what will be Zion. It will all be Zion."[7]

Thus the building of the New Jerusalem will mark the time for the great conversion of the house of Israel, the Lamanites, and the lost tribes, and for the Second Coming of Christ. The exact date is not specified, but it will be before all of these events happen. The building will also fulfill the words of the prophets of both the

Old Testament and the Book of Mormon and will gather a people together in a holy city looking forward to the time of the Lord's Second Coming as foretold by Enoch, the builder of the first city of Zion. (Moses 7:62.) This holy city will be an ensign to the other nations.

10

Jerusalem, A Holy City to the Lord

A major event to precede the Second Coming of Christ will be the rebuilding of Old Jerusalem. The Book of Mormon contains unique prophecies concerning the building of this city. It is to become a holy city to the Lord along with the New Jerusalem.

Ether prophesied that Jerusalem would be "a holy city unto the Lord." He stressed: "It could not be a new Jerusalem for it had been in a time of old; but it should be built up again, and become a holy city of the Lord; and it should be built unto the house of Israel." (Ether 13:5.) The city has existed for thousands of years, but it must be cleansed and rebuilt into a holy city of the Lord. A holy city is a Zion city. The name of the city supports the concept. The word *Jerusalem* means "city of peace," which is one of the conditions of a Zion city.

Joseph Smith also foretold the rebuilding of the city. He said: "Judah must return, Jerusalem must be rebuilt."[1] The word *rebuilt* is significant. To rebuild means to build in the same area as the city of old. Thus, it is the old city that will be rebuilt, not the area *around* the old city, which is what is currently being built up.

Who Will Build the City?

Commenting on Ether's prophecy, Moroni showed that the city will be built into a holy city by members of the Church. He said that when the Jerusalem of old becomes a holy city, the inhabitants will be blessed, "for they have been washed in the blood of the Lamb." (Ether 13:11.) The only way to be washed in the blood of the Lamb is to come to Christ and be baptized with water and fire and the Holy Ghost. (3 Nephi 12:1-2.) Those who are so baptized are added to the Church. (Mosiah 18:17; compare D&C 20:37.) Saying that Jerusalem will be rebuilt by some of her inhabitants who are members of the Church may seem to contradict the teaching that the majority of the Jewish people will accept Christ at the time of his appearance to them. (D&C 45:48-53.) This concern will be cleared up in considering *when* the old city will be rebuilt.

When Will Jerusalem Be Rebuilt?

Although a specific time for the rebuilding of Old Jerusalem cannot be ascertained, there are three events which will help designate the time. As foretold by Isaiah and quoted in the Book of Mormon, the coming forth of the Book of Mormon and the building of the temple in the New Jerusalem in America will precede that rebuilding. Joseph Smith taught us that the third event, the rebuilding of Jerusalem would precede the Second Coming of the Lord.

After prophesying about the coming forth of a marvelous work and a wonder, the Book of Mormon, the Lord said through Isaiah that he would "show unto the children of men, that it is yet a very little while [after the Book of Mormon has come forth] and Lebanon shall be turned into a fruitful field; and the fruitful field shall be esteemed as a forest." (2 Nephi 27:28; Isaiah 29:17.) Lebanon is here used synonymously with Palestine, so the entire territory will become a fruitful field, not just the city of Jerusalem. This will mark the beginning of the fulfillment of the prophecy that the city will become holy.

In a temporal interpretation, this passage refers to the agricultural productivity of the land, similar to another of Isaiah's prophecies that the desert would blossom as a rose. (Isaiah 35:1-2.) As the land blossoms, it is only natural that the city will blossom also. Isaiah prophesied that Jerusalem would be rebuilt after the coming forth of the Book of Mormon. In a spiritual interpretation, since the Book of Mormon will persuade the Jews that Jesus is the Christ (Mormon 5:14), it seems apparent that when the Book of Mormon is taken to the Jews, they will begin to become a fruitful field.[2]

Isaiah saw a time in the last days *"when* the mountain of the Lord's house [temple] shall be established in the top of the mountains." (2 Nephi 12:1-2; Isaiah 2:1-2; italics added.) While many temples have been built in the Rocky Mountains in partial fulfillment of this prophecy, they do not complete it. Isaiah also prophesied that all nations would flow to this temple. The Lord revealed to Joseph Smith that this temple would be built in Independence, Missouri. (D&C 57:3.)[3] The Isaiah prophecy as quoted in the Book of Mormon also says that *when* or after these events take place in the top of the mountains [America], the prophecies concerning Judah and Jerusalem will begin to be fulfilled. Thus a more specific time for the rebuilding of Old Jerusalem is after the temple is built in Missouri.

Joseph Smith said: "Jerusalem must be rebuilt, and the temple, and water come out from under the temple, and the waters of the Dead Sea be healed. It will take some time to rebuild the walls of the city [possibly now rebuilt][4] and the temple, etc.; all this must be done before the Son of Man will make his appearance."[5] When the city will be rebuilt, it may not immediately become the holy city or the Zion city if the majority of the Jews do not accept Christ until after he appears. However, according to Elder Orson Pratt, the temple "will undoubtedly be built [in Jerusalem] by those who believe in the true Messiah"[6] before the Second Coming. Those who believe in the true Messiah will be members of the Church. Therefore, several members of the Church living in the area will build this temple. It need not be assumed that the same people who build the temple will rebuild the city. The majority of the people who have not yet accepted Christ as their Messiah and who are honest and upright may be the ones who will rebuild the city; then it will become a Zion city after they accept their Messiah.

There is one further consideration: the waters that will come from under the temple and the healing of the waters of the Dead Sea are usually associated with the Second Coming, as foretold by other Old Testament prophets. (See Zechariah 14:1-8; Joel 3:17-18.) It appears that all these events will happen soon before Christ's appearance. Thus the Book of Mormon and revelations to Joseph Smith strongly imply that the rebuilding of the city and the temple will take place after the Book of Mormon comes forth and the temple in Missouri is built, but before the Second Coming. The old city may then become a holy city as the inhabitants are converted and live the gospel.

How the City of Jerusalem Will Be Built

The Savior quoted Isaiah while telling the Nephites how Jerusalem would become a holy city. Isaiah, of course, was quoting the Savior. He said: "Put on thy beautiful garments, O Jerusalem." (3 Nephi 20:36; Isaiah 52:1.) For Zion "to put on her strength is to put on the authority of the priesthood" (D&C 113:8), and it seems that Jerusalem's putting on her beautiful garments is a Hebrew parallelism for the same concept. This is supported by the statement "for henceforth there shall no more come into thee the uncircumcised and the unclean." (3 Nephi 20:36; Isaiah 52:1.) The uncircumcised under the law of Moses were those who had not entered into the covenant. Therefore, the unclean can be understood to be the unbaptized. (D&C 84:49-51.) Thus, in any dispensation, Isaiah's statement about Judah's putting on her beautiful garments refers to those who are becoming members of Christ's church. Since the gospel will be taught to Judah, basically by those Jews who have previously joined the Church in America or Europe, the prophecy seems to be describing members of the Church who hold the priesthood coming to Jerusalem.

The next verse of Isaiah, quoted by the Savior to the Nephites, instructs Jerusalem to shake herself from the dust, to arise, and sit down. (3 Nephi 20:37; Isaiah 52:2.) This suggests a cleansing of the city. Historically, Jerusalem has been trodden down by various nations. In the day of cleansing, they are to arise and become independent and then sit down and be established as a holy city. This cleansing is supported from an earlier prophecy of Isaiah, which said that the branch (church) of the Lord would "be beautiful and glorious" to those that are escaped of Israel. Isaiah said further that those who then remained in Jerusalem would be called holy, every one that was written among the living in Jerusalem. This was to follow the Lord's having purged "the blood of Jerusalem from the midst thereof by the spirit of judgment and by the spirit of burning." (2 Nephi 14:2-4; Isaiah 4:2-4.) This may suggest a cleansing by the Lord's judgment and by the outpouring of the Spirit (burning) upon the people.

Old Jerusalem will become a Zion city, a holy city to the Lord and an ensign to the world. This will happen after the Book of Mormon has come forth to the Jews and after temples are built in Jackson County, Missouri, and in Jerusalem. Even though these events will happen before the Second Coming, the city will probably not become completely holy until after the Lord's latter-day appearance to the Jews.

All people will be taught the gospel of Jesus Christ through the Book of Mormon as an ensign. As they accept the gospel and come into the Church, cities of Zion will be built and become holy cities to the Lord and ensigns to the nations. The Book of Mormon is the instrument through which all these things will come to pass. It is indeed an ensign to the nations.

Notes

Preface

1. See *Ensign*, May 1975, p. 65; November 1984, p. 6.
2. *Ensign*, May 1986, p. 78.
3. Joseph Smith, *Teachings of the Prophet Joseph Smith*, selected by Joseph Fielding Smith (Salt Lake City: Deseret Book Company, 1938), p. 71.

Chapter 1

1. There are many references in the Old Testament to the urim and thummim (see Exodus 28:30; Leviticus 8:8; Numbers 27:21; Deuteronomy 33:8; Judges 20:28, 23:9; 1 Samuel 28:6, 30:6-8; 2 Samuel 2:1; Ezra 2:63; Nehemia 7:65).

2. The commandment to not translate the sealed portion is not specifically stated in Joseph Smith's history, but that such a commandment was given is obvious from the Book of Mormon itself and from Martin Harris's visit with Charles Anthon. See Joseph Smith–History (hereafter cited as JS–H) 1:64-66; Ether 3:21–4:7, 5:1; 2 Nephi 27:7-11.

3. While many prophets knew of the coming forth of the Book of Mormon, this work concentrates upon the prophet Isaiah. For verification that other Old Testament prophets knew it would come forth, see Genesis 49:22-26; Psalm 85:10-11; Ezekiel 37:15-20; Habakkuk 1:5; 1 Nephi 19:21.

4. Isaiah also refers to the Book of Mormon as "the law" (51:4) and "sign" (66:19). Furthermore, these prophecies of Isaiah are all associated with the Americas through the designation of "the high mountain" (13:2), "mountains" (18:3), "Zion" (49:14-23), or "isles" (51:5); or by the context of the prophecy (5:26; 11:10, 12; 62:10; 66:19). These interpretations are drawn from the Book

of Mormon, in which many of these Isaiah passages are quoted, and the Doctrine and Covenants. All but Isaiah 18:3, 62:10, and 66:19 are quoted in the Book of Mormon. This work does not give the context of these passages but merely draws attention to the concept. For a fuller interpretation, see the author's work *Great Are the Words of Isaiah* (Salt Lake City: Bookcraft, 1981), which is a chronological commentary on the book of Isaiah. The passages cited are quoted in the Book of Mormon as follows: Isaiah 5:26—2 Nephi 15:26; Isaiah 11:10, 12—2 Nephi 21:10, 12; Isaiah 13:2—2 Nephi 23:2; Isaiah 49:22—1 Nephi 21:22; Isaiah 51:4-5—2 Nephi 8:4-5.

5. The five people to whom these revelations were directed were:

Joseph Smith, Sr., the Prophet's father, who gave encouragement and support throughout the translation and became one of the eight witnesses to the Book of Mormon as a result for that support. (Section 4.)

Oliver Cowdery, who transcribed nearly all of the book as Joseph translated and who became one of the three special witnesses. (Section 6.)

Hyrum Smith, Joseph's elder brother, who gave constant encouragement and support and who became one of the eight witnesses. (Section 11.)

Joseph Knight, a friend of the Smith family, who believed Joseph's declarations concerning his possession of the plates and the work of translation, and who several times gave material assistance to Joseph and his scribe, enabling them to continue the translation. (Section 12.)

David Whitmer, who also became one of the three special witnesses of the Book of Mormon. (Section 14.)

6. See also the Testimony of Three Witnesses in the front of the Book of Mormon.

7. Oliver Cowdery had been told shortly after he began working as Joseph's scribe "that the words or the work which thou hast been writing are true." (D&C 6:17.)

8. The present-day biblical texts contain only two verses of this prophecy (Isaiah 29:11-12), but the Book of Mormon text has a full nineteen verses that describe in much greater detail the bringing forth of the Book of Mormon. That these verses may have once been part of Isaiah's prophecy and not Nephi's commentary, a point not clarified in the Book of Mormon, is indicated by their inclusion in the Joseph Smith Translation of Isaiah.

9. This treatise is not intended to analyze the process of the Book of Mormon translation but merely to show that the Lord verified what Isaiah and Nephi said would happen. For historical verification of the role of Oliver Cowdery as scribe, see Milton V. Backman, *Eyewitness Accounts of the Restoration*, (Orem, Utah: Grandin Book Company, 1983), pp. 97-130.

Chapter 2

1. For a treatise of various Old Testament prophecies concerning Joseph Smith, see Joseph Fielding McConkie, *His Name Shall Be Called Joseph* (Salt Lake City: Hawke's Publishing, 1980). In addition, this work includes a chapter

(8) on "Ancient Traditions of a Messiah Ben Joseph." These traditions speak of two messiahs of the latter days, one a son (*Ben* means "son" in Hebrew) of Judah who will be the Savior of all mankind and the other a son of Joseph who will do a great work in preparing for the Messiah Ben Judah.

2. Brigham Young, *Discourses of Brigham Young*, selected by John A. Widtsoe (Salt Lake City: Deseret Book Company, 1941), p. 458.

3. Joseph Smith, *History of The Church of Jesus Christ of Latter-day Saints*, 7 vols., 2nd ed. rev., edited by B. H. Roberts (Salt Lake City: The Church of Jesus Christ of Latter-day Saints, 1932-51), 5:479-81.

4. *Journal of Discourses*, 26 vols. (London: Latter-day Saints' Book Depot, 1854-86), 7:289-90.

5. *The Saints Advocate*, Oct. 1879, as quoted in Francis W. Kirkham *A New Witness for Christ in America*, 2 vols. (Independence, Missouri: Press of Zion's Printing and Publishing Company, 1951), 1:195.

6. Joseph Fielding Smith, *Church History and Modern Revelation*, 2 vols. (Salt Lake City: Deseret Book Company, 1953), 2:176.

7. *Messenger and Advocate*, Feb. 1835, p. 79.

8. Matthias F. Cowley, *Wilford Woodruff, History of His Life and Labors* (Salt Lake City: Bookcraft, 1970), pp. 100-102.

9. See D&C 86:8-10; 103:17; 110:12; 124:58; 132:30; Abraham 2:11. Many people are under the impression that patriarchal blessings designating the lineage or bloodline of individuals are a declaration of adoption. However, the references cited above establish the literalness of these blessings. There are also dozens of Old Testament prophecies regarding the gathering of Israel from among the Gentiles. See Isaiah 6:13; 10:20-22, 27; Amos 9:8-9; Jeremiah 3:14; Ezekiel 6:8-10; Hosea 1:10-11; 2:23; 3:4-5; 8:8-10; Zechariah 10:6-12. For further confirmation, see Joseph Smith, *Teachings*, p. 151, and Joseph Fielding Smith, *Doctrines of Salvation*, 3 vols., compiled by Bruce R. McConkie (Salt Lake City: Bookcraft, 1954-56), 3:248-54.

10. For a treatise of Isaiah's other prophecies, see Nyman, *Great Are the Words of Isaiah*, pp. 110-13, 176-77, 192, 205-6.

11. The Lord promised Abraham that the literal seed of his body would bear the ministry and the priesthood unto all nations with the blessings of the gospel. (Abraham 2:9-11.) Furthermore, Joseph Smith, Sr., was the first patriarch to the Church, which office belongs to "the oldest man of the blood of Joseph or of the seed of Abraham." (Joseph Smith, *Teachings*, p. 151.) This certainly qualifies Joseph Smith as the person spoken of in D&C 113.

12. "I bless thee with the blessings of thy fathers Abraham, Isaac and Jacob; and even the blessings of thy father Joseph, the son of Jacob. Behold he looked after his posterity in the last days, when they should be scattered and driven by the Gentiles, and wept before the Lord; he sought diligently to know from whence the son should come who should bring forth the word of the Lord, by which they might be enlightened and brought back to the true fold, and his eyes beheld thee, my son; his heart rejoiced and his soul was satisfied and he said; As my blessings are to extend to the utmost bounds of the everlasting hills; as my father's blessing prevailed over the blessings of his progenitors; and as my branches are to run over the wall, and my seed are to inherit the choice land

whereon the Zion of God shall stand in the last days; from among my seed, scattered from the Gentiles, shall a choice Seer arise . . . whose heart shall meditate great wisdom, whose intelligence shall circumscribe and comprehend the deep things of God, and whose mouth shall utter the law of the just . . . and he shall feed upon the heritage of Jacob his father.

"Thou [Joseph Smith, Jr.] shall hold the keys of this ministry, even the Presidency of this Church, both in time and in eternity, and thou shalt stand on Mount Zion when the tribes of Jacob come shouting from the north, and with thy brethren, the Sons of Ephraim, crown them in the name of Jesus Christ." (*Patriarchal Blessings*, book 2, p. 5, as cited in Archibald F. Bennett, *Saviors on Mount Zion* (Salt Lake City: Deseret Sunday School Union Board, 1954), p. 68.

13. In one of the parables of the kingdom, the Savior taught: "The kingdom of heaven is like to a grain of mustard seed, which a man took, and sowed in his field: Which indeed is the least of all seeds: but when it is grown, it is the greatest among herbs, and becometh a tree, so that the birds of the air come and lodge in the branches thereof." (Matthew 13:31-32.)

Joseph Smith gave this enlightening interpretation of the parable: "Now we can discover plainly that this figure is given to represent the church as it shall come forth in the last days. Behold, the Kingdom of Heaven is likened unto it. Now, what is like unto it?

"Let us take the Book of Mormon, which a man took and hid in his field, securing it by his faith, to spring up in the last days, or in due time; let us behold it coming forth out of the ground, which is indeed accounted the least of all seeds, but behold it branching forth, yea, even towering, with lofty branches, and God-like majesty, until it, like the mustard seed, becomes the greatest of all herbs. And it is truth, and it has sprouted and come forth out of the earth, and righteousness begins to look down from heaven, and God is sending down His powers, gifts and angels, to lodge in the branches thereof.

"The Kingdom of Heaven is like unto a mustard seed. Behold, then is not this the Kingdom of Heaven that is raising its head in the last days in the majesty of its God, even the Church of the Latter-day Saints." (*Teachings*, pp. 98-99.)

14. The Hebrew word translated as *ensign* in Isaiah 11 is the same word translated elsewhere in Isaiah as *banner* (13:2) or as *standard* (49:22; 62:10). The use of *standard* in D&C 45:9 is undoubtedly the same.

15. Joseph Smith, *Teachings*, p. 14.

16. *Messenger and Advocate*, April 1835, p. 111.

Chapter 3

1. For a rather extensive list of scripture references to Israel's scattering and subsequent gatherings, see "Israel, Scattering of" and "Israel, Gathering of" in the Topical Guide of the Latter-day Saint edition of the King James Version of the Bible.

2. That this allegory was originally part of the Old Testament is evidenced by Paul's undoubted reference to it in his epistle to the Romans. (Romans 11:11-25.)

3. Joseph Smith, *Teachings*, p. 95.

4. Although it is never called an allegory or a parable in the Book of Mormon, it will be referred to here as an allegory.

5. Joseph Fielding Smith, *Answers to Gospel Questions*, 5 vols., compiled by Joseph Fielding Smith, Jr. (Salt Lake City: Deseret Book Company, 1957-66), 4:203.

6. Jacob bases his prophecy that the Jews will reject the stone that becomes the sure foundation upon the scriptures and is obviously quoting from the plates of brass. While there may have been previous prophecies, the ones known to us from the Bible are Psalm 118:22-23 and Isaiah 28:16. The prophecy was also quoted by the New Testament writers for a similar reason. (Acts 4:11.)

7. Joseph Fielding Smith, *Answers to Gospel Questions*, 4:141.

8. The following list is not exhaustive but verifies that Israel was scattered among the Gentiles: Isaiah 6:13; 10:20-22, 27; 14:1; 24:13-15; 40:9-11; 61:9-11; Jeremiah 3:14; Ezekiel 6:8-10; Hosea 1:10-11; 2:23; 3:4-5; 8:8-10; Obadiah 17-21; Micah 2:12; 4:6-7; Zephaniah 2:1-3; 3:8-20; Zechariah 10:6-12.

9. See D&C 86:8-10; 103:17; 109:60; 113:8; 124:58; 132:30-32.

10. Joseph F. Smith, *Gospel Doctrine*, 5th ed. (Salt Lake City: Deseret Book Company, 1939), p. 115.

Chapter 4

1. This interpretation is supported by Oliver Cowdery's account of the angel Moroni's visit to Joseph Smith. According to Oliver, Moroni said: "Isaiah, who was on the earth at the time the ten tribes of Israel were led away captive from the land of Canaan, was shown not only their calamity and affliction, but the time when they were to be delivered." (*Messenger and Advocate*, April 1835, pp. 109-10.) In other words, Isaiah saw the last days when a remnant of the ten tribes would be delivered from among the Gentiles and restored to the original covenants made to Israel.

2. The traditional interpretation of this passage (Isaiah 49:1-3) and other so-called Servant Songs (Isaiah 42:1-4; 50:4-9; 52:13–53:12) is that it contains praises to the expected Messiah. However, the text of Isaiah 49 says that the servant is Israel. This is further verified in JST Isaiah 41:8-9 and 42:17-25. While some of these so-called Servant Songs may be dual prophecies applying to both the Messiah and Israel (such as 42:1-4 and 52:13-15), the context of the Book of Mormon, as interpreted by Nephi in 1 Nephi 22, shows that the servant is Israel. This is how it is used in this work. For a fuller explanation of these and subsequent verses, see Monte S. Nyman, *Great Are the Words of Isaiah*.

3. The exact date of the apostasy is not known. Although the downfall of the various branches of the church began much earlier than Constantine (see Revelation 2-3), the complete apostasy and the elimination of Church members from the population could have extended for many years.

4. *Journal of Discourses* 18:220. The term *Gentile* has different usages in different time periods. To the Nephites, the Savior defined Gentiles as the people who were taught by the apostles and converted by the Holy Ghost, not by his personal visit. (3 Nephi 16:6.) Following the Savior's ministry, Peter received the revelation to take the gospel to the Gentiles. (Acts 10.) Paul and other apostles subsequently carried the message to the Gentiles in Asia Minor and into Europe. (1 Timothy 2:7; 2 Timothy 1:11.) Thus the Gentiles are the people of Europe and of the United States, which Nephi called a mighty Gentile nation. (1 Nephi 22:7.) The national capacity spoken of by President Woodruff is comparable to Nephi's being a national Jew. (See 2 Nephi 30:4; 33:8.)

5. *Journal of Discourses* 19:229.

6. *Church News*. March 24, 1979.

7. Joseph Smith said, "But few of them [the Gentiles] will be gathered with the chosen family [of Israel]." (Joseph Smith, *Teachings*, p. 15.)

Chapter 5

1. For a fuller explanation, see Joseph Fielding Smith, *Doctrines of Salvation* 1:176-83.

2. Since Isaiah and Micah were contemporaries, and Isaiah seems to have been the head prophet, it is logical that Isaiah was the originator of these prophecies and that Micah recorded them as he did other prophecies of Isaiah. (Isaiah 2:2-4; Micah 4:1-3.) Probably the prophecies quoted by the Savior are no longer in the book of Isaiah because plain and precious truths have been taken away by the great and abominable church. (1 Nephi 13:23-29.)

3. Joseph Fielding Smith, *Doctrines of Salvation* 2:247-251.

4. Joseph Smith, *Teachings*, p. 15

Chapter 6

1. The Book of Mormon prophecies concerning the Lamanites include some of the biblical prophecies that have been lost from the Bible. The list below is almost complete:

   a. Joseph of Egypt. (2 Nephi 3:5-7.)
   b. Zenos. (Jacob 5:24-27, 43-45, 63; Helaman 15:11.)
   c. Isaiah. (1 Nephi 21 [Isaiah 49]; 1 Nephi 22:6-8.)
   d. Lehi. (1 Nephi 10:12-14; 15:12-18; 2 Nephi 3:22-25; 4:3-9.)
   e. Nephi. (1 Nephi 12; 2 Nephi 5:20-25; 25:21; 26:11; 30:3-6.)
   f. Jacob 3:3-9.

g. Enos 1:11-20.

h. Jarom 1:2.

i. Alma (or Mormon). (Alma 3:4-19; 9:14-18, 23-24; 17:11-16; 23:4-7, 17-18; 24:19.)

j. Samuel the Lamanite. (Helaman 15:10-17.)

k. Jesus. (3 Nephi 15:21-24; 21:1-26.)

l. Mormon. (Helaman 3:15; 3 Nephi 2:14-16; 6:14; 4 Nephi 1:17, 20, 38-39; Mormon 5:12-21; 7:1-10.)

m. Moroni. (Ether 8:20-21; Moroni 1:1-4; 9-10.)

2. This accounts for the Lord's revealing to Joseph Smith that the Lamanites were a remnant of the Jew. (D&C 19:27.) It also accounts for the title page of the Book of Mormon. Nephi, however, spoke of the Jews as "them from whence I came." (2 Nephi 33:8.) Thus the Nephites were cultural or national Jews and not bloodline Jews. Lehi's and Ishmael's ancestors were probably among those who left northern Israel when Asa was king of Judah. (2 Chronicles 15:1-10.)

3. In the first two editions of the Book of Mormon, this verse read, "They shall be a white and delightsome people." The 1840 edition, made under the editorial supervision of Joseph Smith, says, "They shall be a pure and delightsome people." This was called to the attention of the First Presidency and the Twelve with the recommendation that the word *pure* be reinstated instead of *white* in the 1981 printing of the Book of Mormon. This recommendation received a strong endorsement by the living prophets, seers, and revelators who preside over the Church today, and it seems to be a better expression of the meaning of the verse.

4. For further support of this concept, see Joseph Fielding Smith, *Doctrines of Salvation* 2:250-51.

5. This may have originally been from Isaiah. The Savior makes no reference to Micah and has both before and after this quotation referred to the fulfillment of the prophecies of Isaiah. Micah retained them as he did others of Isaiah's prophecies. (See note 2, chapter 5.)

6. Joseph Fielding Smith, *Doctrines of Salvation* 2:247-50.

7. See chapter 5.

8. For further verification of this interpretation, see Joseph Fielding Smith, *Doctrines of Salvation* 2:251, and Spencer W. Kimball's address in *Conference Reports*, October 1947, p. 22.

Chapter 7

1. Genesis 49:22-26; Psalm 85:10-11; Isaiah 29; 45:8; Ezekiel 37:15-20.

2. The following prophets, including Jesus, spoke of the Jews in the references cited.

a. Lehi. (1 Nephi 1:4-5, 13, 18-20; 10:2-11; 2 Nephi 1:3-4.)

b. Nephi. (1 Nephi 11:13-36; 15:20; 19:7-15; 20:1-22; 2 Nephi 12:3; 13:1-15; 14:3-4; 15:1-7 [the preceding references beginning with 1 Nephi 19:10

are quotations from Isaiah and other prophets]. 2 Nephi 25:9-20; 29:3-6, 13-14; 30:4, 7; 33:8.)

    c. Jacob. (2 Nephi 6:6-11; 8:17-25 [Isaiah]; 2 Nephi 9:2; 10:3-8; Jacob 4:14-17.)

    d. Amaleki. (Omni 1:15-17.)

    e. Jesus. (3 Nephi 20:29-42, 46 [Isaiah].)

    f. Mormon. (Helaman 8:21-22; 3 Nephi 29:8; Mormon 5:14.)

    g. Moroni. (Ether 13:5, 11; Moroni 10:31.)

    3. See Alma 10:3 and *Journal of Discourses* 23:184. Since the Nephites were literal descendants of Joseph through Manasseh or Ephraim, Nephi's designation should be interpreted as referring to cultural Jews rather than bloodline Jews. However, the Nephites later merged with some literal descendants of Judah who had come from Jerusalem. (See D&C 19:27; Omni 1:13-19; Helaman 6:10; 8:21.) Therefore, there were both literal and cultural Jews after Nephi's time. The Lord designated the Lamanites as a remnant of the Jews in D&C 19:27.

    4. Alma chapters 43-62 deal extensively with the problem of war.

    5. Joseph Smith, *Teachings,* p. 309.

    6. *Ensign,* May 1975, p. 120.

    7. In a reply to Orson Hyde's question about whether "converted Jews are to go to Jerusalem or to come to Zion," Joseph Smith wrote, "I therefore wish you to inform him that converted Jews must come here." (*History of the Church* 4:232.) From the context of 3 Nephi 20 and D&C 133, it seems obvious that the admonition to the Jews to gather to Jerusalem is at the time of their conversion.

    8. The plural *lands* is used because Jacob speaks of the Jews in connection with the promise to all the house of Israel.

    9. Joseph Fielding Smith, *Doctrines of Salvation* 3:70-71.

    10. For an explanation of the Book of Mormon revelations in this text, see Nyman, *Great Are the Words of Isaiah,* pp. 196-97.

    11. LeGrand Richards, *Israel! Do You Know?* (Salt Lake City: Deseret Book Company, 1954), p. 197.

    12. Bruce R. McConkie, *Doctrinal New Testament Commentary,* 3 vols. (Salt Lake City: Bookcraft, 1965-73), 3:509.

    13. Joseph Smith, *Teachings,* pp. 286-87.

Chapter 8

    1. Orson Pratt said that this would be fulfilled when the time of the Gentiles was fulfilled. (*Journal of Discourses* 14:66.)

    2. Joseph Smith, *History of the Church* 1:176, footnote.

Chapter 9

    1. Joseph Smith, *Teachings,* p. 160.

    2. Joseph Fielding Smith, *Doctrines of Salvation* 3:253-54. President Smith's statement includes the statement of Brigham Young.

3. For further verification that Ephraim will administer the building of the New Jerusalem, see Joseph Fielding Smith, *Doctrines of Salvation* 2:250-51.

4. *Journal of Discourses* 11:16.

5. *Journal of Discourses* 26:109.

6. Joseph Smith, *Teachings*, p. 362.

7. *Journal of Discourses* 9:138.

Chapter 10

1. Joseph Smith, *Teachings*, p. 286.

2. For a more complete explanation of this prophecy, see Nyman, *Great Are the Words of Isaiah*, pp. 26-31.

3. See note 1 above.

4. Some Latter-day Saint scholars have assumed that this refers to the building of walls around Jerusalem as it existed at the time of David, not as they are presently built around the city. Time will determine the accuracy of this assumption.

5. Joseph Smith, *Teachings*, pp. 286-87.

6. *Journal of Discourses* 19:20. This interpretation is supported by several other modern-day prophets. See Mark E. Petersen's statement in *Church News*, August 7, 1971. See also Bruce R. McConkie, *The Millennial Messiah* (Salt Lake City: Deseret Book Company, 1982), pp. 279-81.

Index